EUROPEAN MILITARY UNIFORMS

A Short History

EUROPEAN MILITARY UNIFORMS

A Short History

Paul Martin

SPRING BOOKS

Originally published 1963 in German under the title
Der Bunte Rock by Franckh'sche Verlagshandlung
W. Keller & Co., Kosmos-Verlag 7000, Stuttgart.
© Franckh'sche Verlagshandlung W. Keller & Co.,
Kosmos-Verlag 7000, Stuttgart, 1963.
This edition published 1967 by the Hamlyn Publishing Group Ltd,
Hamlyn House · The Centre · Feltham · Middlesex

2nd Impression 1968

Printed in Great Britain by
Richard Clay (The Chaucer Press) Ltd, Bungay, Suffolk

Introduction

Throughout the centuries a nation's distinctive characteristics, attitudes and tastes have been reflected in army uniforms just as in everyday fashions. Naturally the changing demands of warfare have also influenced soldiers' uniforms, but so too has the perennial attraction of bright colours and fancy trimmings. In peace-time there has frequently been an additional motive—personal and social status—and many nations have considered it politic to follow the example of a victorious neighbouring power. In fact, the entire pageant of a nation's historical progress may be studied through the medium of her civil and military uniforms.

The aim of this book is to survey, briefly and concisely, the whole field of military costume from the point when, with the creation of standing armies, it became detached from everyday civilian attire and took on a distinctive guise. Its preeminence lasted until the second half of the 19th century. From then on it became slowly but steadily more drab and neutral, shorn of its rich colours and trappings.

The plates in the book offer a cross-section of civil and military uniforms of every period, in the form of accurate reproductions of contemporary water-colours, prints and coloured lithographs, most of them not easily accessible to the public. It is the author's sincere hope that they will give pleasure to those who are keenly interested in this fascinating branch of history.

A Short History

Man's instinctive urge to cover and adorn himself goes back to primitive times. The gradual addition of coloured accessories such as strips of leather, feathers or ornaments of different colours—worn for the most part on special occasions—paved the way in due course for the introduction of conventional clothing, and later still, costume. This in turn was to be subdivided into dress worn in peace-time, and clothing designed specifically for war. Some of the earliest passages of recorded history provide examples of clothes and ornaments expressing the way of life of a community, particularly among the peoples of the East—Egyptians, Greeks and Romans. But in only a few instances were groups or communities successful in devising a measure of uniformity in dress from which in turn a standard pattern of military attire could emerge.

Thus the development of different methods of combat soon gave rise to a similarity or uniformity in weapons, and this was to lead eventually to uniformity of dress. Princes and nobles dressed their followers and servants in the same colours so as to identify them by their clothing and thereby distinguish them from other social classes.

The combat and tactical methods employed by the Roman legions called for identical equipment within the units, and this equipment, supplied by the State, necessarily made for a certain measure of uniformity in the clothing worn by the legionaries in the 2nd century A.D. This "uniform", however, bore little resemblance to a uniform in the modern sense. It applied only to certain parts of the dress, and to identically coloured cloaks, worn in addition to arms and accoutrements.

Dress and coloured materials, however, did not take on their real significance in war until the end of the Middle Ages. In the 13th century—thanks to the introduction and extension of heraldry—the earliest signs can be seen of a process which was to find its logical outcome and final development in the colourful military costume of modern times.

The banners, standards and pennons of princes and nobles were not sufficient on their own to weld fighting forces together and clearly demarcate opposing sides. It was essential to devise some form of easily identifiable sign, to be displayed on a soldier's clothing, which would at a glance show to which camp he belonged.

The general terms "arms" referred to armorial bearings as well as weapons, and it was by the introduction of "coats of arms" worn by knights and their followers that it became possible by means of badges and colours to distinguish friend from foe.

It was in the 14th century that the art of heraldry burst into full flower. Princes, noblemen and knights arrayed themselves with symbolic badges, designs and colours. Towns

7

and cities were conscious of their power and importance, and with their attendant guilds and corporations adopted standard forms of dress and matching colours. The cloth industry, thanks to the new developments in dyeing techniques, added a further incentive by its capacity to print quantities of cheap, coloured cloth in bulk which prompted the issue of "livery" to officials, servants and soldiers. Indeed, the well-known tri-coloured livery of the kings of France dates back to those times, and was worn, in dark blue, crimson and silver, by the guards of the Royal Household until the Revolution.

By the middle of the 14th century a certain degree of uniformity in the dress of officials and soldiers was already noticeable, while many central European cities, in common with the Swiss Confederates, who were beginning to wear their distinctive symbol, adopted various colour combinations, which, by reason of their heraldic significance, were repeated in the military costume.

The mercenaries in the pay of princes and cities were already dressed in their masters' heraldic colours, and these were displayed particularly in ceremonial processions and military operations in the field.

It must of course be remembered that these were insecure times and fighting was an almost daily occurrence. So arms and equipment had to be supplied in a steady flow, together with military clothing. For example, the city of Nuremberg provided its troops with all-red clothing, while Strasbourg and Paris favoured red and white, and red and blue respectively.

On the other hand, during the 15th century the official trumpeters of some cities—who were often sent out, in the manner of heralds, on confidential missions—were clothed in coloured "liveries", a tradition which persisted until the 17th century.

It is not surprising, therefore, to see the guards of royal houses dressed in luxurious "coats of arms", richly embroidered in appropriate colours, such as King Charles VII of France's Scottish Archers, uniformly dressed in green, white and red, and wearing helmets surmounted by plumes of the same colours.

Shortly afterwards, the campaigns of Charles the Bold of Burgundy, in 1475 and 1477, provided a remarkable opportunity for the supply of uniform clothing, ranging from the Duke's Burgundian Guard, in blue and white, to the Swiss Confederates and their many allies. It is here that we come across drummers, fifers, trumpeters and kettle-drummers dressed in many-coloured heraldic clothing.

The age of the Landsknecht, in the 16th century, introduced the curious fashion for slashed garments, while the Renaissance, with its spirit of daring and novelty, saw a great expansion in the use and application of cloths and other textiles together with a more picturesque and individual approach to fashion. Once again military costume was more closely allied to civilian styles and red was a widely favoured colour.

A captain recruiting a band of mercenaries out of his own pocket could hardly be expected to evince much interest in the clothing of his men. Therefore every individual dressed much as he pleased, at his own expense, the only common symbol being a badge, worn by choice rather than by order, such as the white cross of the Swiss and French, or the red cross of the Germans and English. This, apart from their "war cry", was the only distinguishing feature, for even their head-dress consisted of a barret-cap, or béret, of their favourite colour, generously decked with coloured plumes.

It was around this time, in 1506, that what was to become the Swiss Papal Guard marched into the Vatican to the strains of fife and drum, uniformly clothed in *divisas*.

Contrary to popular belief, neither Michel-angelo nor Raphael were the founders of that colourful costume which inspired the design of a uniform still in existence to this day. The basic colours of this uniform—blue, gold and red—go back to the luxurious livery of the Medici. It is interesting to note that Church Beadles (called *Suisses* in France) carry out their functions in many parts of the

8

Plate 1. Prussia, 1779. Officer of Hussar Regiment von Zieten No. 2 (*left*), von Czettritz No. 1 (*centre*) and von Rosenbusch No. 3 (*right*).

Notes on this and following plates will be found at the end of the book on pages 93–128.

Prussia, 1779. Hussars of Regiment von Zieten No. 2 (*left*), von Czettritz No. 1 (*centre*) and von Rosenbusch No. 3 (*right*).

Plate 2, page 11. Above: Austria, *c.* 1762. Infantry and Artillery.

Below left: Prussia, 1757. Infantry. Officer of Fusilier Regiment Prince Frederick-Francis of Brunswick No. 39.

Below right: Prussia, 1786. 1st Guards Battalion No. 15. Officer and grenadier.

Plate 3, page 13. Above left: Württemberg, 1787. Russian Hussars of the Guard.

Above right: Württemberg, 1787. Horse Grenadier.

Below left: Russia, *c.* 1762. Grenadier of the St. Petersburg Division.

Below right: Russia, *c.* 1762. Infantry Officer.

Plate 8, page 23. Switzerland, *c.* 1793. Major of the 1st Basle Dragoons.

Palatinate-Bavaria, 1783. Dragoons, Officer and Dragoon.

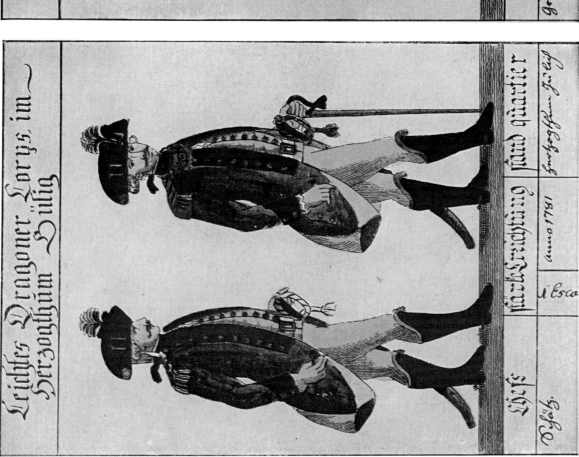

Plate 4. Palatinate-Bavaria, 1783. Light Dragoons, Officer and Dragoon.

Plate 5. Württemberg, 1785. Foot Guards. Officer and private.

Württemberg, 1785. Artillery. Officer (*left*), Grenadier (*centre*) and Fusilier (*right*).

Austria, 1820. Hungarian Noble Guard.

Plate 6. Austria, 1790. Galician Noble Guard.

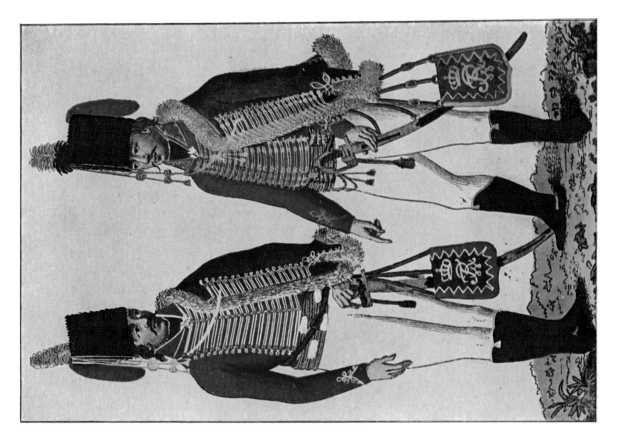

Prussia, 1800. Officer and Hussar of the Magdeburg Hussars.

Plate 7. Prussia, 1786. Officer and Hussar of the Prince Eugène of Württemberg Regiment.

Franz Feyerabend fecit.

Tragoner Officier
Contin.t Basel

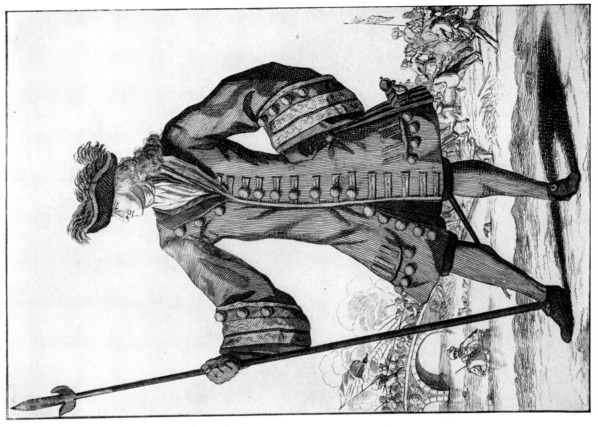

Brandenburg, 1700. Ensign of the Foot Guards.

Plate 9. France, 1722. Captain of *Cent-Suisses.*

Plate 10. Hessen–Darmstadt, *c. 1786.* Grenadiers.

Plate 11, page 29. Right: United States, *c. 1776.* Soldier of the Militia.

Americaner Soldat.

Accurate Vorstellung eines americanischen Soldaten, von einem Baÿreüschen Officir welcher sich
dermalen in America, in Englische Dienst befindt, gezeichnet und heraus geschickt worden. Ihre
Kleidung ist von Zwilch, sie habe lange Gewehr und Bajonet, u. seind sehr dauerhafft u. gesund.

Joh. Mart. Will exc. Aug. V.

Plate 12. France, *c.* 1740. Dragoon on Forage Patrol.

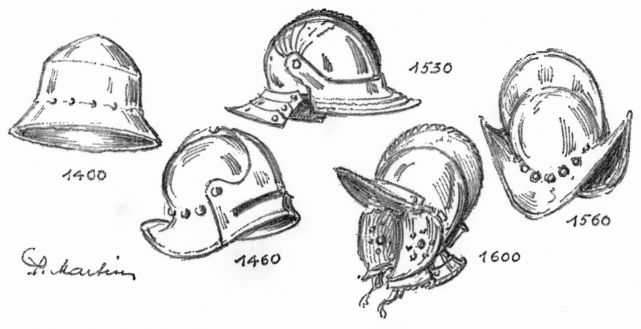

Sallets, iron and crested helmets.

world to this day in similarly coloured uniforms.

Spanish fashions exerted a powerful influence at the end of the 16th century and the beginning of the 17th century, contrasting strongly with preceding styles. Austerity was the rule for court dress, tightly fitting hose, small waist and back slightly hunched—almost in the shape of a hump—this feature being reproduced even in suits of armour. Spain was then the leading civilised country in Europe, and her fashions were obediently followed. From this time onwards formations of guards of various European courts took part in the royal ceremonies—wearing the colours of their sovereigns, but in costumes which were directly influenced by the Spanish style.

It was in the second quarter of the 17th century at the beginning of the Thirty Years War (1618–48), that the court fashions of Paris and Vienna began to make their impressions on costumes and were once more reflected in military attire. Now the soldier made his appearance in a buff coat or jerkin,

wide, baggy trousers, coloured stockings and on his head a broad-brimmed hat, turned up at one side. A cuirass for the foot-soldier and a suit of armour—still in its complete form for the horseman—completed the protective armament.

Schiller, in his famous play *Wallenstein's Camp*, gives a picturesque and colourful description of that period. In spite of wartime hardships, privations and shortages (witness, for example, Callot's celebrated engravings), it was nevertheless an age in which new fashions were introduced and exemplified in royal courts throughout Europe. But naturally as far as military costume was concerned practical considerations produced a number of variations on the ruling fashions for civilian dress.

Troops of many nations were now drawn by the course of events to central Europe, Germany in particular. French, Italians, Spaniards, English and Scots, Hungarians and Poles, all made their distinctive national marks on the military sartorial scene. Although high-ranking officers were distinguished by

D

coloured sashes, varying from nation to nation, the rank and file—more often than not a "brutal and licentious soldiery"—contented themselves with civilian clothing stolen or looted in occupied territory.

It was with the appearance of Gustavus Adolphus's well-disciplined troops in 1632 that a new and colourful note was struck in the midst of all this chaos of contemporary warfare. Indeed, the Swedes served as models for all belligerents, for their "Blue", "Yellow" and "Green" regiments (so called from the colour of their clothing and not from their ensigns) represented the first real step towards uniformity of dress in the field. At the same time the design of weapons was standardised, which naturally led to increased efficiency.

With the Peace of Westphalia in 1648 civilian fashions began to exert a powerful direct influence on military dress, and this inter-dependence was to be strongly evident for many years. Leather gave way to coloured cloth, in coarse material for the rank and file and finer quality for the officers. Full armour was discarded and replaced by the cuirass worn by the heavy cavalry, pikemen and most of the officers of all ranks. The breast-plate, finally reduced to its smallest expression as the gorget, remained in service for officers during the whole of the 19th century and is even occasionally seen today.

At this time more attention was paid to the attire of the trumpeters and kettle-drummers, who were dressed in bright and colourful clothing based on the livery of their superiors. The long, false sleeves extending down the back and lavishly adorned with lace then became the distinctive feature of military instrumentalists.

In the heyday of Louis XIV's reign Paris became the undoubted centre of fashion and was to exercise a marked influence far beyond the frontiers of France. France's ascendency in fashion lasted to the end of the 17th century.

Military costume now adopted the civilian dress of the day, with its ample coat and wide sleeves covering the sleeved waistcoat and thus taking the place of an overcoat. The use of the overcoat was now restricted to the cavalry, affording both rider and steed some protection from the weather.

Meanwhile, in England, Oliver Cromwell had as far back as 1645 recognised the fundamental need for a uniform dress for his parliamentary army, and it was he who introduced scarlet as the basic colour for his soldiers' clothing. This is still the colour associated with British regiments on ceremonial occasions. The Scots, on the other hand, have retained their traditional national costume.

At the beginning of the reign of Louis XIV the British Army was already uniformly clothed in red, except the Artillery and the Royal Horse Guards—the "Oxford Blues"—who wore dark blue. In France the French and Swiss troops of the royal guards paraded in the royal colours of blue with red and white. But no distinctive pattern of military clothing had yet emerged.

Some of the French Household troops had already been issued with a common garment, for example, the mounted *Grands Mousquetaires*, who wore the celebrated dark blue sleeveless jacket, laced and embroidered in silver, and bearing, on front and back, a silver flaming cross. The same sleeveless jacket, but in red cloth, was adopted by Cardinal Richelieu's Guards. Yet the clothes worn underneath these jackets were still dictated by individual choice, reflecting variants of contemporary styles.

The *Cent-Suisses* (the Hundred Swiss) Bodyguard, raised in 1497, retained for ceremonial purposes the ancient dress of the Swiss Landsknecht. This was worn until the French Revolution, then discarded and later reintroduced at the Restoration. This palace guard, charged with the personal security of the sovereign, was imitated by the courts of Prussia, Spain, Saxony and Lorraine.

Following the example of Gustavus Adolphus, there is no doubt that Louis XIV, with the help of Louvois and Colbert, and aided by the evolution of the textile and dyeing industries, made a considerable contribution

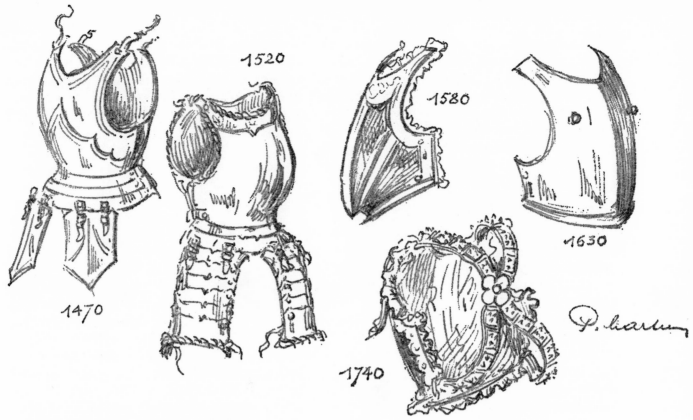

Armour for foot-soldiers, breast plates and cuirasses.

to the standardisation of dress in the French Army. The first regulations and ordinances were promulgated by Louvois after 1674, and the Peace of Nijmegen in 1678. Uniform, in the modern sense, was born.

From about 1680 onwards the various branches of the French Army were distinguished by the basic colour of their garments: either blue or red for the household troops and guards, or grey, buff and (later) white, for the Royal or French regiments. Units of the other armies also adopted characteristic colours—red in the case of the Swiss and Irish, blue for the Germans and others. In order to distinguish the regiments a special colour was chosen for the coat-linings, thus producing collars, cuffs, waistcoats and breeches of an individual and distinctive appearance. But although the rank and file now wore uniform, officers were not to renounce for many years yet their individually selected clothes, cut from expensive materials and closely modelled on prevailing fashions.

With the introduction of standing armies, however, coloured military dress—in other words, uniform—became firmly established, governed henceforward by its own laws.

In the second half of the 17th century, as the theatres of war shifted eastwards, the influence of Hungarian and Polish national costume began to make itself felt, while peculiarities of dress, characteristic of some Slav peoples—the Croats and Pandours, for example—also left their mark. Indeed, in some cases there were even traces of Turkish influence.

The "hussar" light cavalry had already made its appearance, dressed in laced dolmans and pelisses. They had gained a fearsome reputation for speed and ruthlessness, fighting alongside the Slavonic border troops during the Thirty Years War.

Yet only at the beginning of the 18th century do we come across regular corps of hussars, in the pay of Austria and France. Their characteristic dress, which was to be imitated all over the world, enjoyed universal popularity until the first World War.

Of course, new designs in costume and fashion were not always dependent primarily

35

Coats of arms (Burgundy), cassock and sleeveless jacket (French).

on practical necessity. Very frequently royal commands or regulations laid down at high level led to certain innovations or had the effect of checking excessive variety in styles. Such regulations were chiefly intended to curb extravagances in court dress and official costume, with particular emphasis on manorial and hunting liveries, then much in vogue on the Continent. It was at this period that shoulder straps came into being, designed originally to prevent the cross-belt from slipping over the right shoulder, but eventually becoming the distinguishing mark of an officer's rank, as well as an ordinary ornament of dress.

This was a change based on simple utility, but very often a new fashion could be created by mere chance. For instance, when Marshal Luxembourg was unexpectedly attacked by Prince William of Orange at Steenkirk Camp in 1692 the confusion was such that the French officers had no time to dress, nor even to tie their cravats. Many simply flung these around their necks and pushed the lace-ends through a button-hole of the waistcoat. Thus

a new fashion was born—cravats *à la Steenkerque*—which enjoyed immediate popularity at court and in the army.

It is time to take a look now at the development of uniforms in other continental countries.

Very gradually, the neighbouring nations followed the example set by France, and the armies of the Holy Roman Empire, with Austria in the lead, began to introduce military uniform around the year 1700. Here white became popular as the basic colour for coats cut from a cloth which was still coarse in texture, while Bavaria, Württemberg, Brandenburg and Saxony drew their inspiration either from France or Austria or, alternatively, devised their own.

Thus we find that around the beginning of the 18th century the army of the Elector Maximilian Emanuel of Bavaria (the "Blue King") was attired in sky-blue; the Elector of Brandenburg preferred dark blue, while the troops of Saxony were dressed predominantly in red and white. Here again in the cut of the clothes as well as in general appearance

36

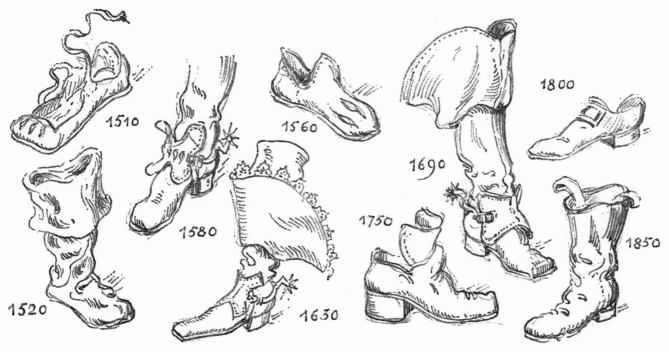

Military shoes and boots.

contemporary civilian fashions were closely followed, apart from the additional details of dress and equipment necessitated by particular weapons and current tactical requirements.

For example, it became customary to turn up the brim of the hat to facilitate arms drill and firing, and thus the cocked hat was born. Or again, when they were actively engaged in throwing grenades the grenadiers would replace their hats by a plain worsted cap, and this soon became the typical head-dress for grenadiers and *élite* troops.

The crown of the cap, now stiffened and surmounted by a tassel or pompon and further adorned with bearskin, was soon adopted in central and southern Europe, while in Prussia and allied countries it was fitted with a brass plate, displaying armorial bearings, and became the celebrated mitre cap. The cavalry, cuirassiers and dragoons had from the middle of the 17th century already adopted, in place of a hat, an iron helmet fitted with a nosepiece and a broad scaled neck-cover.

This uniform dress, plain to start with, soon came to be ornamented with button-holes in a contrasting colour and embellished with lace. This smart outfit was regarded as an incentive for soldiers who had been pressed into service, not always on a voluntary basis, and undoubtedly it played a part in promoting *esprit de corps*.

All officers, according to rank, covered their coats with gold or silver lacing, and this highly elaborate form of personal adornment became general everywhere, lasting until the end of the century. Gorgets and sashes were an essential part of an officer's wardrobe, and the skills of the lace-maker and embroiderer produced masterpieces of design and craftsmanship.

Yet all this splendid and colourful display, now reaching its culmination, was not simply an indispensable part of reviews and ceremonial parades. The practical test of coloured uniforms was on the battlefield, where, amid the thick clouds of smoke emitted by the fire-arms of that period, uniforms would clearly stand out in their tactical positions. During the 18th century we come across numerous examples of changes in the colours adopted for military dress. Some of these alterations were occasioned by new governments ushering in different styles of dress at court, and these were extended to household troops and sometimes to military uniforms in general. Thus certain colours took on definite political significance—a tradition which has persisted to the present day.

Furthermore, the conclusion of an alliance might very well produce a change in dress by encouraging a close imitation or even a direct copy of a particular uniform, as, for example, during the Seven Years War among the pro-Prussian states such as Württemberg, Hesse-Kassel, Brunswick and others.

In a sense, even religious conviction could influence the choice of colours in certain armies. Thus Catholic states, such as Austria and France, for example, showed a preference for white, while Protestant countries, such as Prussia, her allies and the northern countries, favoured a predominance of blue. There were exceptions of course—Great Britain and Denmark kept to red and Russia retained dark green.

Apart from France and Austria, who were slow to follow the general trend, Brandenburg—or rather Prussia—soon took the initiative in bringing about a development which occurred in the various continental countries and finally produced its own rules and standards, owing very little to civilian fashions of the day.

The fashion of amply cut clothes with wide, loose cuffs extending to the elbow was still prevalent; stockings were of coloured wool, and head-dresses took the form either of a large cocked hat, a bearskin cap or the grenadiers' mitre-cap with an embossed plate in front. The hair, worn long, was soon to be "clubbed" in a bag, while officers favoured a full-bottomed wig.

In 1688 the Elector Frederick William III of Brandenburg, imitating the dazzling example set by the Sun King, ordered a copy to be made of the Mousquetaires' sleeveless jacket for the *Trabantenleibgarde*, his body of mounted palace guards.

Apart from the hussars, the cavalry— cuirassiers, dragoons or horse-guards and grenadiers—followed the general trend set by the foot-soldiers. Arms and equipment were closely adapted to current military needs and improvements, while the artillery, still regarded as a separate entity, displayed a preference for dark tones.

There were rules and regulations, down to the minutest detail, covering the external appearance of military uniforms. This meticulous "gaiter-button" mentality, so characteristic of the Prussian Army, was now very common.

Other curious incidents also brought about changes in military costume. In 1717, for example, Augustus the Strong, Elector of Saxony, a sovereign of expensive tastes, exchanged about 600 men, cuirassiers and dragoons, with Frederick William I of Prussia, for a magnificent service of china vases from the palace of Charlottenburg.

The bartered soldiers were then formed into a regiment of Prussian dragoons and dressed in sky blue and white uniforms similar to the main colours of the china. In this manner the "China Dragoons" made their appearance, while the costly chinaware, now in Dresden, became known as the "Dragoon Vases".

In Brandenburg-Prussia the emergence of the wool and cloth industry, although restrained by a policy of strict economy on the part of court and state, inevitably exerted a pronounced influence on the development of military uniforms. With the accession of the young King Frederick William I in 1713, the cut of military dress became tighter and narrower so that the close-fitting Prussian uniforms took on a distinctly different appearance from the French style then in vogue.

The "Soldier King" soon introduced new reforms with his battalion of Giant Grenadiers, and these set the pattern for the entire Prussian Army and other armies as well. The blue coat was shortened to the knee, while waistcoats, collars, lapels, cuffs, breeches and stockings were in contrasting red. These stockings were later replaced by white gaiters with brass buttons. Hair was dressed and tied with a ribbon in a long queue extending to

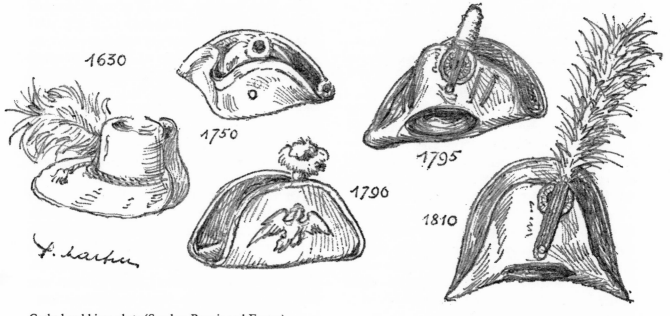

Cocked and bicorn hats (Sweden, Prussia and France).

the waist, and there was a red and blue cloth mitre-cap, decoratively embroidered in gold. The red stock then became the attribute of young qualified recruits.

In France, Austria and Great Britain the familiar roll of the drum, sometimes accompanied by the fife, was swelled out by the addition of other military musical instruments, and the players' uniforms were elaborately trimmed with lace and braid. Most popular of all were little Negro boys who served either as kettle-drummers or, decked out in their rich eastern dress and turbans, played the percussion instruments in the "bands of musick"—a custom, incidentally, which survived until the middle of the 19th century. It was about this time that "wings" or "swallows'-nests" replaced epaulettes on the musicians' uniforms.

In 1740 the army of the young King Frederick II of Prussia made its appearance. In addition to the reputation it acquired for fighting qualities, its general smartness and air of efficiency soon became a model for the armies of neighbouring powers.

In sharp contrast to the austere and parsimonious policies of his father, the young King fitted out his Foot- and Horse-guards with uniforms lavishly trimmed with lace, showing a personal preference for silver rather than gold embroidery, although gold was retained for the units raised during his father's reign.

The luxurious full-dress uniform of the *Garde du Corps* calls to mind an anecdote told by the well-known adventurer, Baron Frederick von der Trenck, in his memoirs. "I was in charge of the guard of honour," he wrote, "on the occasion of the wedding festivities for the marriage of Princess Ulrike of Prussia in 1744. At the spot where the crowd was thickest an urchin cut off the back of my crimson velvet *soubreveste* (sleeveless jacket) with its fine silver embroidery . . . which later gave rise to all kinds of jokes on the theme of the 'plucked' orderly officer."

Units of Uhlans (whose name in Polish means "horsemen in Tartar dress") first appeared in Prussia in 1741. Their distinctive colours were white and sky-blue. Their

39

uniform was copied in France by Marshal de Saxe's *Volontaires Tartares*, and in 1745, again in Prussia, under the name of Bosniaks, they formed a nucleus for all the future Uhlan regiments.

At this period, Hussar units of every nation wore the busby, or high-crowned *mirliton*, with its distinctive band. These units were identified by various patterns and colours of braiding. Dolmans, pelisses, saddle-cloths and sabretaches were decorated in a colourful medley of yellows, chestnuts and blacks.

In Prussia the "Death's Head Hussars", raised in 1741, gained immediate renown by virtue of the famous emblem which was to become their own special badge. According to an old tradition, this emblem had its origin in the funereal trappings used at the burial of King Frederick William I.

Field officers in Austria, France and Prussia showed a particular fondness for saddle-cloths and pelisses of panther or leopard skin to offset the glittering array of their full-dress uniform. The Hungarian Noble Horse Guards were in fact using these right up to the collapse of the Dual Monarchy in 1918.

The assembled troops at ceremonial parades and reviews or even on the field of battle must have made a vivid and colourful picture. In those days, of course, it was vital for general staffs to be able to identify the various units under their command, and van Blarenberghe's painting of the Battle of Fontenoy in 1745 strikingly illustrates this point: the different regiments, like a magnificent carpet, seem to form a multi-coloured pattern amid the smoke and confusion of battle.

It was at the Battle of Rossbach in 1757 that Frederick the Great, surveying the field of operations, exclaimed, "What are those red walls which my artillery cannot breach?" To which an aide-de-camp replied, "Sire, those are the Swiss Regiments of Planta and Diesbach." Speechless with admiration, the King raised his hat.

The ordinary soldier soon began to take a pride in the special regimental features and distinctions of his uniform, which were mainly conveyed by differences in the pattern and position of the braid and lace. His self-respect and *esprit de corps* were greatly enhanced, and the costume which he had often been compelled by force to wear was transformed into a badge of honour. He was proud to wear the King's uniform, and whereas he may previously have regarded himself as mere cannon fodder, he was now frequently inspired to devotion to duty, even to the extent of supreme sacrifice.

An episode in 1760, involving Prussia's fine Anhalt-Bernburg regiment, illustrates this point. The indifferent bearing of the regiment at Dresden aroused the King's anger, and officers and men alike were deprived of all distinctions, such as lace and braiding, a particularly degrading punishment. But honour was regained by the regiment's heroic conduct at the Battle of Liegnitz, and the distinctions were restored ceremonially, to the great pleasure of all ranks.

Soon afterwards other principalities, such as Brunswick, Hesse-Kassel, Hesse-Darmstadt, Württemberg and Baden, followed the Prussian example: and after the Seven Years War, France, Great Britain, Russia and Sweden all drew their inspiration from the Prussian model for their uniforms and equipment.

Now, more than ever, uniform became the object of numerous rules and regulations, attention being paid to the most minute detail. Here, for example, are some extracts from the "Warrant for the Battalion of the Grenadier Guards of His Most Serene Highness the Landgrave of Hesse-Darmstadt . . . in Detailed Paragraphs", dated 1749:

"Para. 1.—All officers are requested to see that the soldiers appear perfectly turned out in clean shirts and stocks, their hair dressed and powdered, and leatherwork pipe-clayed.

Plate 13. Left: France, 1779. Alsace Infantry Regiment (German).

Right: France, 1779. Dillon Infantry Regiment (Irish).

Left: France, 1779. Royal-Allemand Cavalry.

Right: France, 1779. Bercheny Hussars.

ALSACE. Nº 54.

DILLON. Nº 90.

ALSACE. Nº 54.

DILLON. Nº 90.

Plate 14. France, 1780. Royal French Guards (*left*).
Royal Swiss Guards (*right*).

France, 1780. Life Guards (*left*). Gendarmes of the
Guard (*right*).

Plate 15, page 45. France, 1796. Volunteer of the
Army of the Rhine.

Volontaire venant de l'Armée du Rhin. d'Ulm.
dessiné d'aprez nature le 20 Oct: 1796.   5.me detachep.t
par Zix.

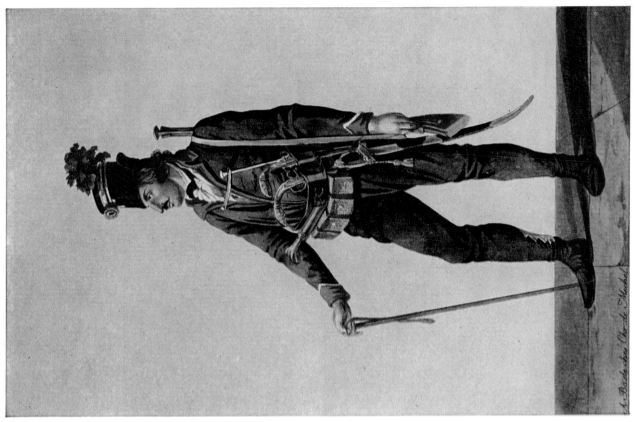

Austria, 1793. Officer of Wurmser's Free Corps.

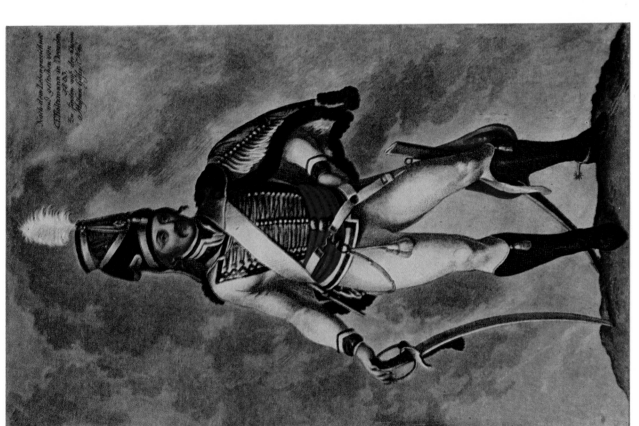

Saxony, 1803. Hussar from the Saxon Regiment of Hussars.

Plate 16.

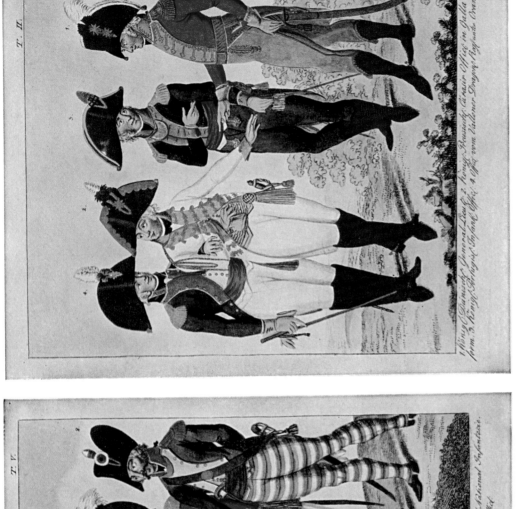

Plate 17. Europe, *c.* 1802. Officers (Infantry): 1. Prussia, 2. France, 3. Denmark, 4. Hanover.

Europe, *c.* 1802. Officers (Cavalry): 1. Denmark, 2. Prussia, 3. Portugal, 4. Holland.

Plate 18. Great Britain, *c.* 1803. Naval Artillery. From left to right are shown: three gunners, one officer laying a gun, a subaltern and two sailors.

Plate 19. France, *c.* 1805. Horse Artillery.
In the centre a *Chef d'Escadron*, on the right a gunner, between
the two an artillery-driver; in the foreground a trumpeter
masks another gunner in a frock coat.

Plate 20, page 55. Right: France, 1805. Dragoon in marching
order.

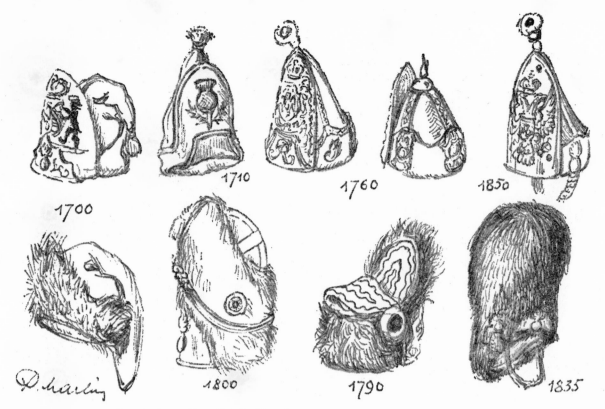

Grenadiers' mitre caps: Brandenburg, Great Britain, Prussia, Russia. Bearskins: France, Austria-Hungary, Great Britain.

"Para. 2.—On parade, hair must be cut in regulation manner and rolled in seven curls, well-combed and always powdered.

"Para. 3.—Hair is to be tied, two fingers from the head, in a ribbon forming a queue, and this must reach down to the small of the back. Strict cleanliness is imposed on the men. They must wash their hands and face, and keep their body perfectly clean in order to avoid being covered in vermin . . . moustaches will be waxed and kept in position overnight by means of a tie. . . .

"Para. 4.—Waistcoats and breeches will be pipe-clayed in white and not yellow, and thoroughly brushed before parade in order to avoid soiling the cloth coat.

"Para. 5.—On service, the grenadiers' mitre-cap . . . will be well fitted and secured to the head, not inclined over the neck, but correctly tilted to the front, above the nose."

These few extracts will serve to show the lunatic hold of fashion on contemporary military costume.

Meanwhile, Marshal de Saxe, in France, had introduced the "classical" dragoon helmet, with a turban, crest and horsehair streamer. It was copied in Great Britain, Hanover and Hesse-Kessel, and was adopted, around 1780, by the light cavalry of the young republic of the United States.

At about the same time it was adopted as the standard head-dress for the Fire Guards of the City of Paris and was later to become the typical helmet of Parisian firemen. In due course this helmet served as a pattern for all the fire brigades in France, Italy, Spain and other countries.

As the rationalisation of military uniforms progressed, towards the end of the 18th century, so other civic organisations on the Continent began to issue their personnel with uniform clothing—for example, the Postal and Customs authorities and the police. Some of the private postal organisations also provided their employees with their own uniform. The *Postillons de France* wore blue and red, the Thurn and Taxis organisation in Germany favoured yellow and blue, while the

F

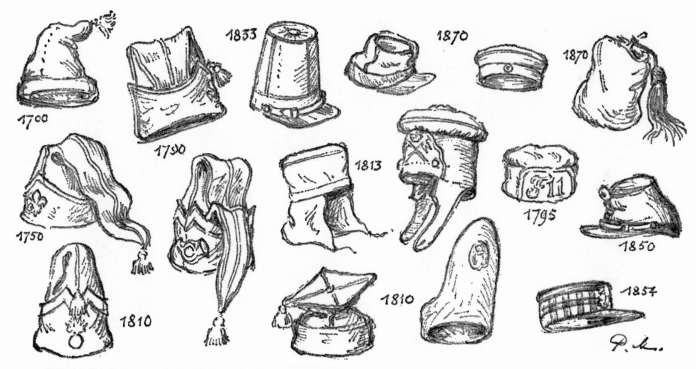

Forage caps, bonnets and miscellaneous headgear of different armies.

Bavarians turned out in sky-blue and black laced with silver, etc., etc.

Around the end of the 18th century, miners' corporations adopted special clothing for their members, different for every rank. In Silesia and Saxony especially, the whole hierarchy was clearly distinguished by costumes of varying designs and colours.

In the many spectacular reviews and ceremonial parades which Parisians witnessed shortly before the Revolution, there was little to choose between the Swiss Guards (the "Beetroots") and the French Guards (the "Blue Bottoms") as far as smart appearance was concerned.

The Swiss Guards, in their red uniforms with blue facings and silver lace, were massacred when the Tuileries were stormed and plundered. The monarchy was overthrown, and with it disappeared a world of elegance and colour, of glittering parades and uniforms. An age of courtly refinement and exquisite taste vanished for ever.

The political upheavals of the time had world-wide repercussions, and the field of military costume was only one of many aspects of national life on the Continent which was profoundly affected.

Prussia had already carried out innovations in the reign of Frederick William II by producing clothing and equipment of a more practical design. Even in Russia, as far back as 1786, the Empress Catherine II had sanctioned a type of uniform common to all branches of the army; a fact, incidentally, which may well have been a first step towards those better conditions which were not to find any practical application until the beginning of the 19th century. The introduction of long trousers fitted with leather leggings for the infantry as well as the cavalry was a welcome improvement, as indeed was the new head-dress with its fur crest and peak, and the abolition of the plaited queue. This, however, was restored a little later by Paul I, who was a great admirer of Frederick the Great and his army.

In the meantime, the French Revolution of 1789 had led to the creation of the volunteer National Guard in Paris and other French

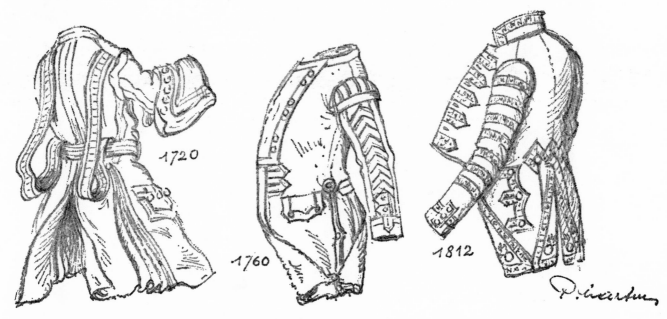

Trumpeter's coat (Bavaria), drummer's coat (Prussia) and musician's uniform (France).

towns. They were fitted out in an attractive uniform—dark blue coats with white lapels and turnbacks, and red piping, collar and cuffs—a uniform which was to symbolise the momentous years to come.

During the wars of the Revolution, with the hostility between the "Blues"—the inexperienced volunteers—and the "Whites"—seasoned veterans of the old royal army—the white coat finally disappeared, about 1796, from the assortment of different uniforms worn by the various French units. The wide trousers of the Revolutionaries, with their coloured stripes, soon ousted the knee-length white breeches.

Prussia had begun to dress her troops in these cotton trousers a little earlier in order to protect or even replace on active service the white and yellow breeches which were worn with white or black gaiters in full dress. It was not long before the *Sansculottes* (the "No-Breeches") achieved renown far and wide by defeating troops which were obviously hampered by the outmoded "spit-and-polish" mentality of the time.

The traditional tricorn hitherto used by all armies was gradually being modified into a two-cornered hat, and this underwent further rational alterations after 1880. Some infantry and light cavalry units in France had already adopted a fur-crested helmet: Bavaria followed suit in 1789 with the so-called "Rumford" helmet, then Württemberg and later Austria, around 1800.

At about the same time the Hungarian busby, or *mirliton*, was transformed by a slight broadening of the top into a cylindrical shako with a detachable peak and fitted with a plate, braid-hangings and plume. This was first seen in Prussia in 1805, then in France in 1807, and finally in Prussia and Austria, subsequently becoming the standard form of head-dress for all units.

There was a spirit of emancipation in the air during the early years of the new century, and the abolition of powdered hair and queues, with the new fashion for short hair, was one clear sign of it. Only a few units of the Guard remained faithful to the old fashion of plaited hair.

59

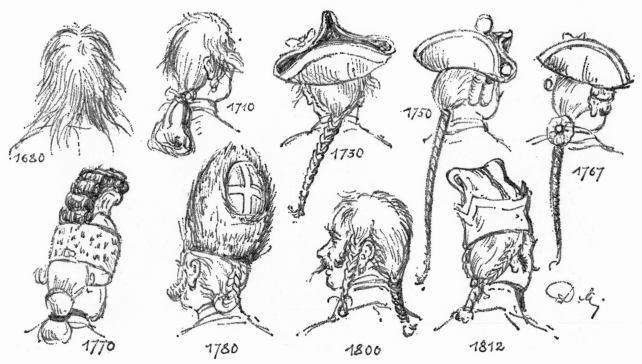

Military head-dress and hair styles, France (1680–1812), Prussia (1750).

The Napoleonic era, prelude to the most far-reaching reforms, set the pace for a new style in military uniforms. However, the tactics of the age still entailed "battle formations" involving rapid and accurate identification of the opposing forces. This is why as late as 1812 some troops still marched into battle in all the splendour of full dress.

The dazzling and spectacular uniforms of the famous Imperial Guard were not surprisingly imitated by other countries, particularly the magnificent Polish Lancers, the *Chasseurs à Cheval*, or again the curious Mamelukes in their eastern dress inspired by the Egyptian campaign.

Military costume entered a new era of colourful pageantry, initiated by France in 1794, when the whole Continent followed suit, but with pride of place still going to the French.

The Cuirassiers abandoned the cocked hat for the "classical" helmet fitted with a bearskin turban, vertical plume and crest with horsehair streamer protecting the neck, while hats remained the prerogative of generals and officers of all ranks. After the Revolution the rank and file of infantry wore the crossed leather equipment which soon became general and lasted until the middle of the last century.

In Poland, Kosciuszko's volunteers had become famous, and their national costume spread rapidly to other countries, chiefly through the medium of the Polish corps then in the French service. Indeed, the *czapka* and the *kurtka* eventually became the standard clothing for lancers throughout the world.

With the creation of the Confederation of the Rhine, along with the defeat of Prussia and Austria, France again pointed the way on the Continent, while Russia and Great Britain followed their independent paths in the field of military costume and design.

Broadly speaking, this consisted of coats with open skirts, subsequently cut square at the waist, and tight sleeves. Prussia introduced long trousers fitted with numerous brass buttons. These were much to the liking of King Frederick William III, although Napoleon considered them ridiculous. Nevertheless, they were adopted by the French

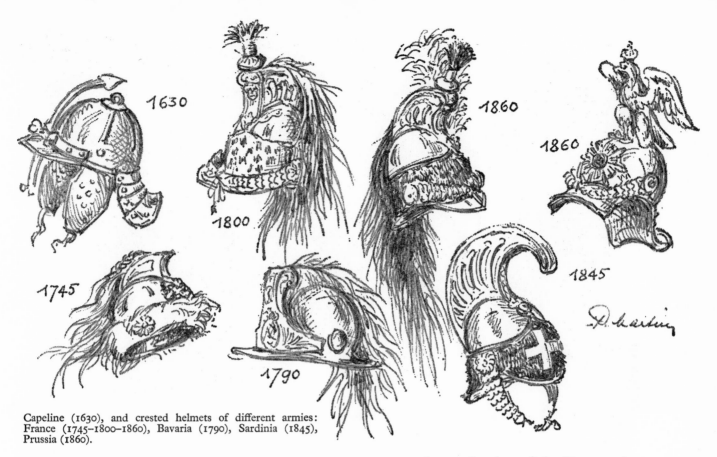

Capeline (1630), and crested helmets of different armies: France (1745–1800–1860), Bavaria (1790), Sardinia (1845), Prussia (1860).

hussars and *Chasseurs à Cheval* in marching order.

In order to distinguish the various ranks of field and junior officers, France, as early as 1762, had introduced epaulettes in gold and silver for officers, and a little later in worsted for other ranks. About 1800 these were in general use in the armies of her allies.

Space does not permit a detailed description of all the national and local variations of army costume prevalent at this time. But it is worth remarking upon the custom of dressing the bands and drummers in "reversed" colours, or even in completely different uniforms, a tradition which prompted many commanding officers to give consent to the most colourful and extravagant sartorial displays, as can be seen when one looks at pictures of those fantastic drum majors swaggering at the head of their regiments.

One can readily appreciate the amusing account given by the artist Albrecht Adam in his *Memoirs of a War Artist* of an incident which he witnessed in 1812 in Russia, near the River Duna. "I watched," he wrote, "the constant coming and going of the Emperor's marshals on the banks of the river. It was there that I had an amusing experience. I noticed an important individual dressed in a sky-blue coat covered in gold lace, with gold-laced scarlet trousers, and wearing a curious hat covered with plumes; in other words, a figure which I could not quite place. Strangest of all was that he kept walking about very near the Emperor, who, in common with his retinue, was on foot. Finally, I approached an officer standing near me. 'Tell me,' I said, 'who is that extraordinary drum major in whom His Majesty is so interested?'—'*Mon Dieu*,' replied the officer. 'That is Murat, the King of Naples.' "

During the Russian Campaign and the ensuing wars the Cossacks—a light cavalry in the literal sense—burst on the scene. Their national costume was imitated by, among others, the Cossacks of the Guard in Prussia, and their distinctive style of dress had a widespread influence on military fashions.

A common sight on the roads and on the

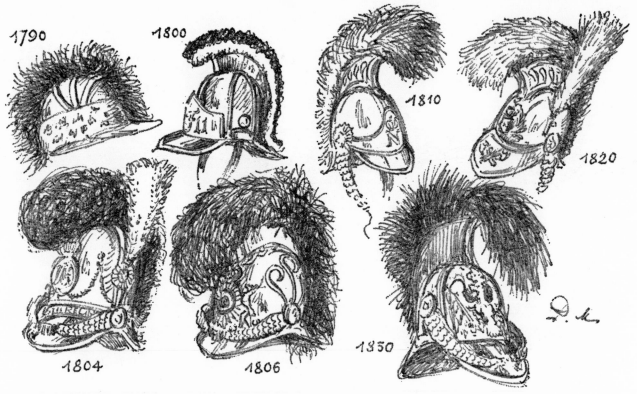

Crested helmets: France (1790–1810–1820). Austria, (1800), Bavaria (1804), Württemberg (1806), Prussia (1850).

actual field of battle were those hardy indomitable women, the sutleresses, who tended the wounded and shared in all the hardships of active service. Their bright and cheerful costume, made up from miscellaneous items of military attire, stood out in colourful contrast to their drab surroundings. Later, especially in France, they could be seen, gaily dressed in uniform, marching at the rear of their regimental bands.

France's continental blockade directed against Great Britain had some unexpected consequences. The textile industry, for example, was affected. Indigo, an indispensable dye for uniforms, became so scarce that Napoleon decided to dress his troops in white. His decisions on such points of detail may have been influenced by political considerations as well. It is reported that the sight of white uniforms covered in blood on the battlefield of Eylau made such an impression on the Emperor that he immediately decided at whatever expense to revert to the traditional blue for his troops.

At the same time there was war at sea. The crews of warships were already wearing sensible and practical working clothes which came to be accepted as regulation dress. It was 1830 before a distinctive naval uniform made an appearance. Great Britain and the Netherlands had considerable influence in this respect, and the familiar blue clothing, wide collar, black scarf and oil-cloth cap were eventually adopted by sailors of all nations.

The importance of tradition may be illustrated by a typical example in Great Britain. When queues and plaited hair were abolished in 1808 the Royal Welsh Fusiliers were stationed in the British colony of Nova Scotia. Neither officers nor men were prepared to conform to the new regulations for short hair, so that clubbed hair and queues remained in fashion for a number of years. The regulation was eventually imposed, but as a protest the officers of the regiment continued to wear a knot of black ribbon at the base of the collar, which became traditional, being first sanctioned in 1834 and then in 1900 as a distinction for all ranks.

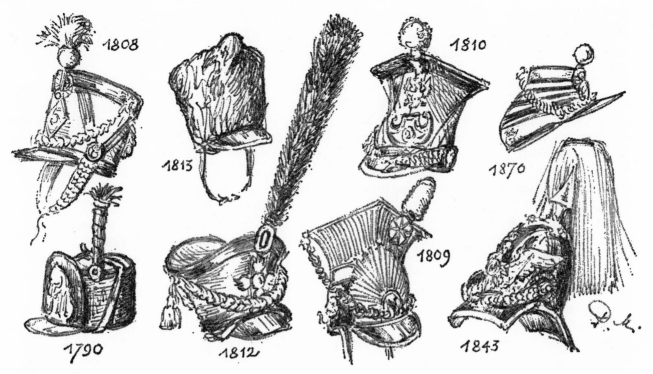

Shakos, Tchapka and Pickelhaube: France, Prussia, Poland, Spain, Austria, Russia, Poland, Prussia.

As from 1808, the reorganisation of the Prussian Army had resulted in a number of innovations in costume based to a large extent on the Russian model. The introduction of a shako for the foot-soldiers and of a crested helmet for the heavy cavalry then set the pattern for most of the other German states.

With the growth of resistance movements in the German universities against the Napoleonic régime, a sign of a new fashion appeared in 1806. This took the guise of a black uniform, worn by the volunteer units raised in Brunswick in 1809 and by Major Lutzow's "Black Corps" in 1813. In most cases it was simply a military adaptation of the long double-breasted tunic worn in the student societies—a shift in emphasis made all the easier by reason of the prevailing military mentality in civilian circles.

All the reserves of army clothing and equipment were pressed into service, and even some 17th-century helmets appeared on the scene, suitably adapted and repainted, in Krokow's Volunteer Corps, while green became finally established as the traditional colour for all rifle units.

The Treaty of Paris in 1815 ushered in a period in which military uniforms were to flourish in all their dazzling multi-coloured glory, now that utilitarian battle dress could once more give way to more decorative ceremonial garb. The general style was tight cut and elegant, while head-dresses assumed gigantic proportions, topped by the most fabulous plumes.

It was now becoming increasingly commonplace for uniforms to be introduced in many branches of the civil service, for example, the postal authorities, customs officials and police. Both in design and colour, such uniforms had a pronounced military flavour. Later still the railwaymen followed suit, choosing varying shades in the darker colours. In France they were even issued with side-arms in the early days. It would hardly have been surprising therefore to see a sentry present arms in all good faith to a postman in a gold-laced uniform!

Altogether it was a happy, peaceful interval

63

in European affairs, and the appearance of national guards in their colourful uniforms, parading to the strains of military music, gave rise to admiration rather than alarm. The ladies, of course, had always had a weakness for a smart uniform, and the appearance of soldiers could be guaranteed to cause emotional havoc in any garrison town. An officer's prestige was enhanced by his gold and silver epaulettes and shoulder knots, and the flattering style of military tailoring enabled him to cut a fine figure indeed.

Between 1820 and 1850 there was a marked relaxation in the body-tight cut of the coat, and France again took the initiative by introducing the traditional red trousers in 1829, which, incidentally, acted as an important boost to the textile trade. These red trousers were worn till 1914.

During the German war of independence against Napoleon, a light cap without a peak, corresponding to the British forage-cap, had begun to replace the heavy regulation shako or helmet, especially in camp. This fashion spread and even outlasted the first World War.

The experience of French troops campaigning in much warmer climates, such as in Spain (1823) and Algeria (1830), made it vital to reduce the sheer weight of military clothing and adapt it to new conditions. One innovation was the peaked képi, a sensible substitute for the heavier shako.

Some units, such as the Zouaves, deliberately assumed a costume of African design, with baggy trousers and the *chéchia* for head-dress, an example soon followed by the native troops, Algerian infantry and Spahis, about 1834.

The year 1831 saw the appearance of the famous *Chasseurs d'Afrique*, mounted on their magnificent Arab horses. They were dressed in sky-blue and primrose yellow, with red trousers, wide and leather-protected, a feature to be imitated soon afterwards by most other cavalry units, not only in France but also in Russia, Austria and other countries.

In 1838 several battalions of *Chasseurs à Pied* were formed in France on the pattern of the celebrated Tyrolese *Kaiserjaeger*. They wore a dark blue tunic faced with primrose yellow, a képi or shako for head-dress, and blue trousers. Spain and Sardinia followed the French model.

Prussia, now the leading military power on the Continent, proceeded in 1843 to revise its military equipment, introducing a single-breasted tunic, an example followed immediately by northern countries such as Denmark, Sweden and Russia. Great Britain, however, did not make the change until after the Crimean War. Cross-belts were discarded in favour of a waistbelt, the equipment being carried by a system of braces.

At the time when the Swiss were engaged in bitter wrangling, at Basle, over the introduction of the képi in place of the shako, Prussia was adopting the legendary *Pickelhaube*, a helmet of excellent protective quality which made its way through Europe as far as Russia, and even reached the United States. It became the typical symbol of the Prussian or German soldier, and disappeared about 1915-16.

The 1st Regiment of Prussian Foot Guards had, in 1824, followed the Russian pattern by re-introducing the high-fronted brass mitre-cap, which lasted for some ninety years. In France, the Latin countries, Great Britain and Austria the full-dress bearskin cap for grenadiers remained in force, and indeed can still be seen today in such countries as Great Britain, Sweden and Denmark.

Plate 21. Austria, 1805. Hussars, Regiment of Hessen-Homburg No. 4 in marching order.

Plate 22, page 67. Austria, c. 1805. Infantry and Artillery.

Plate 23, page 69. Austria, c. 1805. *Chevaulégers*. Regiment Hessen-Homburg No. 2.

Plate 24, page 71. Above: Prussia. Officer and private of the King's Regiment No. 18, c. 1800 (*left*). Officials of the Water and Forestry Department (*centre*) and Post Office, 1787 (*right*). Below left: Prussia, 1806. Carabinier of the 2nd Regiment of Hussars von Rudorff. Below right: Prussia, 1806. Non-commissioned officer of Grenadier-Battalion von Reinbaben.

Plate 25, page 73. Prussia, 1806. Officer of the Garde du Corps Regiment.

Leib Husaren Regt Rudorff
Präsentiert das Gewehr

Grenad: Unterofficier vom Bataillon Reinbaben Regt Zirsch
Präsentiert das Gewehr

Officier vom Regt. Garde du Corps.

Plate 26. French troops at Lübeck, 1806.

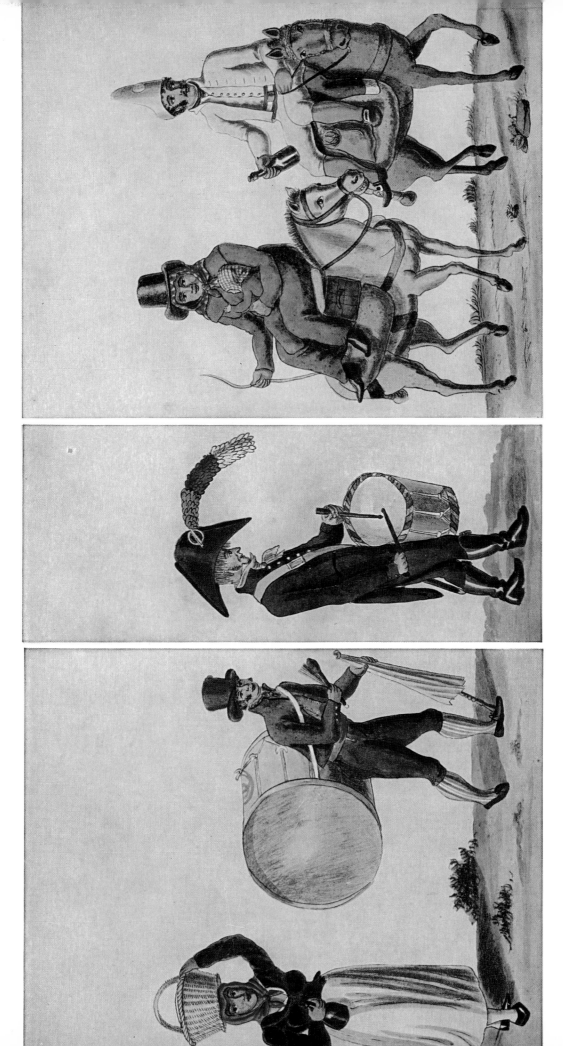

Plate 27. Spain, 1807. Sutleress and musician of the Catalonian Infantry Regiment.

France, c. 1810. Drummer of the Customs Service.

Spain, 1807. Trooper of the Algarve Regiment with his wife.

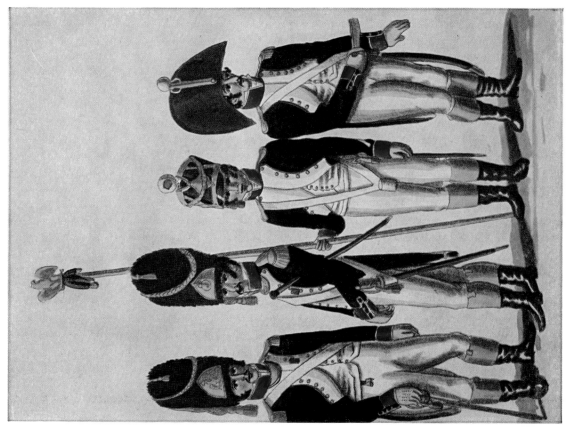

France, 1812/13. Officers and Eagle-bearer of the 93rd Infantry Regiment.

Plate 28. France, 1812/13. Dismounted Cuirassiers in Hamburg.

Plate 29. France, 1813. Seamen on the Alster at Hamburg.

France, 1812. *Chasseurs à Cheval, élite* company.

Plate 30. Holland, *c.* 1810. 6th Infantry Regiment at Hamburg. From left to right: Grenadier pennant-bearer of the 2nd Battalion, Officer of grenadiers, two pioneers, Drum-major, fifers of fusiliers and grenadiers.

Plate 31, page 85. Kingdom of Westphalia, 1810. Lieutenant-Colonel of the *Garde du Corps* in full dress.

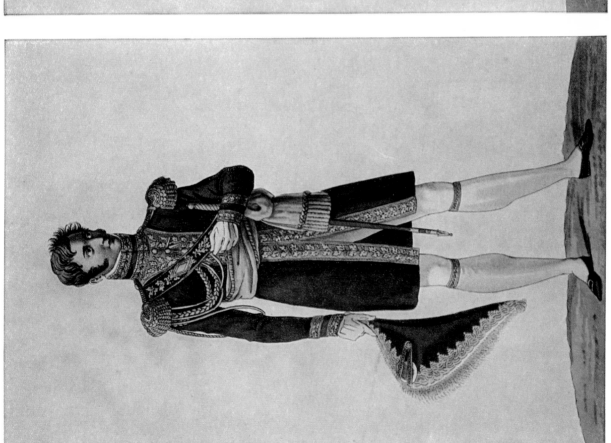

Plate 32. Kingdom of Westphalia, 1810. Captain-General of the Guard in levée dress.　　　Kingdom of Westphalia, 1810. *Chasseur-Carabinier.*

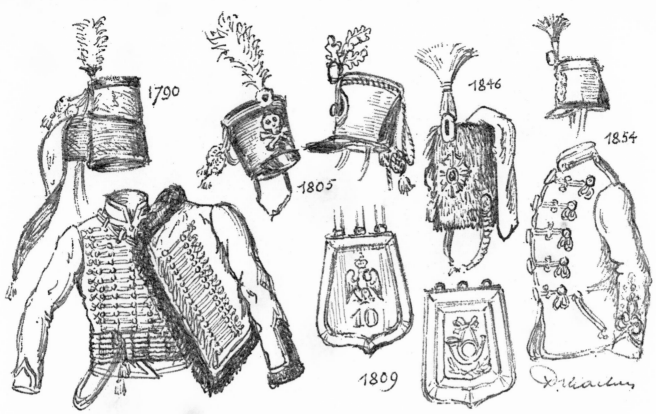

Hussar clothing and equipment: France, Prussia, Austria-Hungary.

Prussia's example was then followed by the confederate states of Germany, apart from Bavaria and Württemberg, who retained their individual qualities. Bavaria kept to her traditional sky-blue uniform with fur-crested helmet, while Württemberg stuck to dark blue with shako or small busby. Austrian troops still wore their white tunics, while, until the first World War, the Hungarian infantry retained their tight blue trousers fitting into the boots and decorated with coloured lacing at the seams.

The universal military reorganisation which had taken place in Europe by creating standing armies had led, in Prussia, to the concept of "people in arms" (*Volk in Waffen*). More than ever, uniform had now become a cloak of honour, a symbol of general admiration and esteem, and a criterion of tailored elegance the world over. However, uniform then began to break away from the dictates of general fashion, to be governed more specifically by the laws of tradition and military history. Two typical examples were the Prussian's guard-lace (*Gardelitzen*) and the so-called "bear's-paws" (*Barentatzen*) worn as cuff slashes by the Hungarian grenadiers.

It is a fact that the prototype created around 1840–50 became basic until 1914, although various details of uniform may have suffered a number of alterations. From that moment a general concern for a form of military dress more in keeping with the exigencies of modern warfare finally led to a distinct separation between full-dress for ceremonial occasions and field service dress proper.

The various revolutionary movements which shook Europe in 1848 and 1849—in Germany, Austria, Hungary, France and Italy—had grave and lasting consequences. Once again, political change was reflected in contemporary fashions, both civilian and military. A number of popular leaders who emerged at this time succeeded in introducing revolutionary new styles among the ranks of the various National Guards, Civil Guards and Volunteer Corps whom they led into battle. In Baden, Hecker's followers, with their large plumed hats and open-necked

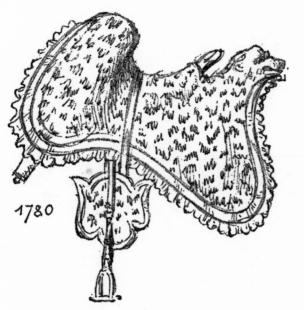
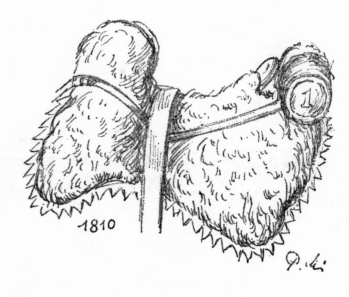

Saddle cloth of French Hussars, officer and trooper.

shirts, initiated a style far removed from the Prussian ideal of rigid formality: and in Italy, Garibaldi's famous Redshirts struck a similarly informal note.

Yet the morale of the standing armies of the Continent owed much to the jealously preserved traditions linked with their uniforms. It was not unusual therefore for a soldier to develop a deep attachment towards any special distinction, such as the red plume frequently worn by trumpeters, or the "back badge" of the Gloucestershire Regiment.

Some of these peculiarities may still be seen in certain uniforms derived from national costumes, for instance, the Scottish Highlanders in their kilts or the Italian Bersaglieri in their round plumed hats. Another striking example is the characteristic white dress of the Greek Evzones, the design of which is completely in keeping with national tradition.

Coloured uniforms still made their distinctive mark on the battlefield. There is the famous example of the "thin red line" of the Sutherland Highlanders, checking and beating back the advance of Russian cavalry at Balaclava, in 1854. Sometimes, however, a coincidence in the use of certain colours produced the very opposite effect required. Thus, during the Italian campaign of 1850, the Piedmontese infantry opened fire on the French Lancers of the Guard, mistaking their white coats for those of Austrian cavalry.

Meanwhile, a new Imperial Guard had been formed in France, built upon the traditions of the First Empire and rivalling its illustrious predecessor in luxury of clothing and equipment. In fact, this was another era of splendour and showmanship, as all the courts of Europe tried to outdo one another in the magnificence of their guards' uniforms.

The impressive ceremonial dress of the *Cent-Gardes* on guard at the Tuileries attracted sight-seers from many lands, and their frozen immobility gave rise to many an amusing incident. The same inflexible position is adopted to this day by the British Brigade of Guards on sentry duty.

The Tsars also dressed their guards in sumptuous uniforms, tastefully designed,

90

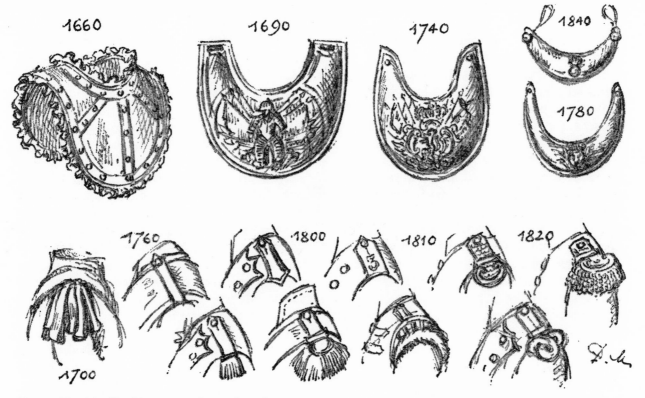

Gorgets (France)—Shoulder-straps, wings and epaulettes.

during the latter part of the 19th century, and these were much admired by connoisseurs.

This was all very well for ceremonial occasions, but in the field, at the mercy of rain, snow and cold, these fine uniforms in their bright colours became dulled and tarnished, so much so that they were often unrecognisable, as happened in the Crimean War of 1853–54. Both the Confederates and the Union troops in America during the Civil War of 1861–65 had adopted a uniform based upon the French pattern, and volunteer units were particularly attracted by the Zouave costume. Later, however, Great Britain exerted a much stronger influence on American army fashions.

But as the demands and methods of warfare changed, so too was the design of military uniforms gradually becoming swayed by practical considerations rather than the dictates of fashion. Lighter clothing and equipment for the soldier was now the general rule in France and then in Germany. In France and other Latin countries canvas gaiters were worn over the trousers and boots, while the

Prussian troops acquired the habit, during the Danish campaign of 1864, of wearing their trousers inside the boots, a fashion which was soon copied, around 1870, by the whole of Germany.

There were always exceptions to the rule, factors which made for slackness in the strict observance of dress regulations. For example, the breakdown of normal supply routes might make it necessary to improvise, and in France particularly a sudden whim on the part of officers and other ranks alike often resulted in modifications which later became permanent. Sometimes faults in dyeing could lead to a regulation colour undergoing subtle variations in shade. At other times, especially in occupied territory, use would be made of any available supplies of cloth. A remnant found in store would be used as a stopgap, and troops might be seen in the field wearing outlandish costume far removed from regulation dress. In the Egyptian campaign of 1799, for instance, French troops took the field decked out in eastern fabrics of the most garish colours, bearing not a trace of

91

resemblance to the standard uniforms in which they had disembarked.

Another example was the brown cloth, found in the Spanish convents, which was used extensively for making breeches and trousers for the French occupation forces during the Peninsular Wars of 1809 to 1812.

As far as the cloak or the infantryman's greatcoat were concerned, there were civilian styles up to the campaigns following the French Revolution, and these remained optional under the Empire except for the Imperial Guard. It was not until the 1812 Regulations that the greatcoat became a compulsory garment in winter. Even so, it was worn in colours ranging from beige to dark grey, in distinct contrast to the white or blue cloaks of the cavalry.

While Great Britain retained a basic colour of scarlet for most of her uniforms, the Continent, with the northern alliance of Prussia and the other German states, and Denmark, Sweden, Norway, France, Spain and Italy, adopted a dark blue for their tunics, with facings of various colours. Russia alone remained faithful to her dark green.

Austria finally gave up her traditional white uniform in 1868, but the facings in a variety of different shades remained unaltered. The Austrian cavalry were fitted out with red trousers, which resulted in a panorama of many colours which the Viennese flippantly called "H.M.'s Paint-Box" (*k.u.k. Farbkastel*).

At the concerts given by the massed military bands of Europe at the Paris International Festival of 1867 the range of uniforms must have made a brilliant and glittering spectacle indeed. The drums, fifes and full bands of all nationalities played alongside under the baton of the famous Wieprecht, then Director of Music of the Prussian Guard. This was probably the swan-song of colourful military splendour on a grand ceremonial scale. Three years later the Franco-Prussian War broke out. Full-dress uniforms disappeared on both sides, to be replaced by field service kit. This was the end of the splendid uniforms of Napoleon III's Imperial Guard. It was the austere Prussian model which became general.

It was inevitable that colours more suitable for work in the field should displace the bright and varied uniforms of earlier years. Protective colourings, such as khaki, iron-grey, sky-blue, etc., were produced to protect the soldier and submerge him as much as possible in his surroundings, even to the extent of rendering him invisible at a distance.

Yet colourful military uniform was not quite dead. Fortunately, despite everything, full dress saw yet another revival. Today it still holds its own in ceremonial parades and military displays, retaining its close link with historical tradition and gladdening the hearts of countless people everywhere who still respond to the magic appeal of military pomp and circumstance.

Notes on the Plates

Illustrations on the front end-paper:

Austria. Chart of the Imperial and Royal Army, Leipzig, 1792.

This chart is of a type widely used by all the leading military powers from the middle of the 18th century onward, showing at a glance, in tabular form, the uniforms worn by the various units of an army. This particular one illustrates the uniforms of the Imperial troops of 1782, whose dress at that time was governed by regulations of 1767.

The often subtle differences of colour in the facings are clearly defined, and the name and locations of each regiment are shown.

In 1798 the upright collar was sanctioned, and in 1800 the existing headgear was replaced by the crested helmet for cavalry and infantry.

Illustrations on the back end-paper:

Detail of a coloured drawing made in 1796 by von Mühlen, showing in diagram form the Prussian Army under Frederick II, as well as the newly formed regiments and battalions.

The intention of this chart was to show the various alterations to military uniforms which occurred between 1786 and 1796. The costume of the Cuirassiers and Hussars underwent no alterations, and although the dragoon uniforms are shown partly in white, this development never actually took place.

These charts were very popular in the second half of the 18th century, although their accuracy is sometimes suspect. On the other hand, they contain much useful documentary information and are undeniably very decorative.

Plate 1

Prussia, 1779. Officers (*above*) and Hussars (*below*) of Regiments No. 2 (von Zieten), No. 1 (von Czettritz) and No. 3 (von Rosenbusch). Enlarged reproduction from an anonymous MS album in the Print Room at Berlin-Dahlem.

The Hussars shown here are in the conventional hussar dress, but certain regimental peculiarities are recorded with meticulous attention to detail. Thus, the Hussar in Regiment No. 2 is mounted on a horse whose harness is decorated with shells. The officer's charger has red harness with shells. All the officers have richly embroidered sabretaches and saddle-cloths (note particularly the shape of the saddle-cloth in Regiment No. 3).

The points of the saddle-cloth were liable to become discoloured through soiling, and other illustrations dating from 1758 show them rounded.

All the officers depicted here are wearing coloured fancy breeches, liberally embroidered.

Plate 2

Above: Austrian soldiers, *c.* 1762.

This anonymous coloured drawing shows a group of characteristic types during the Seven Years War period.

On the left, an infantryman of the border regiments wearing the equipment peculiar to these troops as well as the typical red cloak.

Next, a soldier of the Colloredo Regiment (so-called "German" infantry) with a foot-soldier from a Hungarian regiment.

The grenadier, with bearskin cap and laced facings, belongs to Harsch's Regiment. The gunner, on the right, is recognisable from the curious basic colour of his coat, known as "wolf-grey".

Below left: Prussia, 1757. Officer of Fusilier Regiment No. 39 (Prince Frederick Francis of Brunswick). Copy of a Saxon MS, made about 1757, the property of the Museum für Deutsche Geschichte in Berlin.

Below right: Prussia, 1786. Officer and grenadier of the 1st Guards Battalion No. 15. Engraving from the album of Prussian uniforms by C. C. Horvath, Potsdam, 1789.

These two plates illustrate the changes of fashion which took place during the last thirty years of Frederick The Great's reign. While the officer (*left*) still wears the long waistcoat and a coat with a very small collar, the officer of the Guard (*right*) wears a larger tricorn: the waistcoat is shorter and the coat already shows signs of a more open fitting.

The very simple uniform of the 39th Regiment forms a sharp contrast with the lavish silver-laced coat of the Battalion of the King's Guard. The tricorn, with its broad lace and plumes, was originally intended for general officers only.

Plate 3

Above: Württemberg, 1787. Russian Hussars of the Guard (*left*) and Horse Grenadier (*right*). Coloured drawings taken from a MS on the Württemberg troops by Rischmüller, 1785.

Whole of the left-hand figure shows one of the many varied uniforms of the 18th-century Ducal Guard (doubtless the First Company); the Horse Grenadier on the right belongs to the corps raised in 1758, which took part in the Seven Years War. At that time the cuirass was worn under the coat, and the bearskin cap had no plume. This uniform was discontinued in 1790.

Below: Russia, *c.* 1762. Grenadier of the St. Petersburg Division (*left*) and Infantry Officer (*right*). Coloured drawings taken from an album of the Russian Army *c.* 1762.

On the accession of Peter III, the uniforms assumed the same style as the Prussians', but with green as the basic colour. The regimental distinctions were not subject to regulation, and often depended on the whim of a commanding officer.

The grenadier is shown in a sleeved waistcoat, without his dark green coat, which would, in summer, be carried in the regimental transport. The officer, on the other hand, is depicted in full dress, with his blue and gold sash and gilt shoulder strap.

From 1763 the colour of the coat was altered to light green, with all facings red.

Plate 4

Electorate of Bavaria-Palatine, 1783.

Left: Officer and Dragoon of the Light Dragoon Corps of the Duchy of Jülich.

Right: Officer and Dragoon of La Rosée Regiment. Coloured engravings from the album by E. Trieweiller, Captain in the Palatine Regiment Leopold of Hohenhausen, 1783.

The Light Dragoons, in a chasseur-type uniform, were raised in 1781 and disbanded during the wars of the French Revolution.

The Dragoons wore a red coat from 1683, which was superseded by a white uniform in 1785. La Rosée

Regiment was dismissed in 1789 on the re-organisation of the Dragoon Corps, of which only two units remained.

Plate 5

Above: Württemberg, 1785. The uniforms depicted show an officer and other rank of the Württemberg Foot Guards in 1785, from a drawing by Rischmüller, 1785.

This 300-man unit was inspired by the Guard of Frederick II of Prussia (see Plate 2).

Below: Württemberg, 1785. The artillery are dressed in the basically sky-blue uniform which replaced the red after the middle of the century. The sky-blue uniform remained typical of the artillery until 1817.

Plate 6

Left: Austria, 1790. Galician Noble Guard in Gala Uniform. Coloured engraving by Schütz, Vienna, 1790.

Right: Austria, 1820. Hungarian Noble Guard in Gala Uniform. Engraved by Heinrich Mansfeld, Vienna, 1820.

These two figures typify the luxurious uniform worn by the Court Guards of Their Imperial and Royal Majesties. The influence of national costume is clearly perceptible.

The Galician, or Polish, Guard was raised in 1782, but was disbanded as early as 1790. Raised in 1760, the Hungarian Noble Guard lasted until 1918. The uniform shown here, based upon the national colours of green, red and white lavishly adorned with silver trimmings and a leopard-skin, was worn with various contemporary modifications until its disbandment in 1918. At the end of the 19th century it was dismounted.

Plate 7

Left: Prussia, 1786. Hussar Regiment No. 4 (Prince Eugène of Württemberg). From the Prussian Army album by C. C. Horvath, published at Potsdam, 1789.

The uniform worn by the officer and other rank of this unit, raised in 1740 under the name of Natzmer's Uhlans, is typical of the latter years of Frederick the Great's reign. They wore the mirliton until 1770, and later had the braiding of their jackets enclosed in a lace framework, a common fashion in the last third of the century. Plumes were introduced in the summer of 1762 for all the Prussian cavalry, the free corps, rifle corps and general officers.

Right: Prussia, 1800. Magdeburg Hussars. After the album published by G. L. Ramm, Berlin, 1800.

This unit dates its origin from the escort raised in 1761 for Prince Ferdinand of Brunswick and transferred in 1763 for similar duties to Prince Henry of Prussia at Rheinsberg. Dressed originally in blue dolmans and yellow pelisses with white braiding, the corps was in 1761 given the uniform shown here, which was also adopted by Prince Henry's escort in 1778. Both corps were mounted on greys and wore blue cloaks.

They were later separated, and the former was disbanded after the capitulation of Magdeburg in 1806. The latter, renamed the Berlin Hussars in 1802, were disbanded in 1808.

Plate 8

Switzerland, c. 1793. Dragoon Officer of the Basle Contingent. Hand-coloured engraving by Franz Feyerabend, from the set of twenty-six types of the Confederate contingents at Basle (Basle Historical Museum).

Franz Feyerabend (1755–1800) worked at Basle as a monochrome artist and engraver. He was the author of a valuable series of prints, drawn from life, representing the diversity of uniforms worn between 1792 and 1797 by the various Swiss Confederate units manning the frontiers of their country.

Daniel Merian, portrayed as the Major commanding the First Basle Dragoon Regiment, wears silver shoulder-cords and epaulettes denoting his rank. In the background are troops with a standard-bearer and a drummer wearing a white coat with red facings, whose drum is decorated with flames in the Basle colours of black and white. The Colonel's groom wears a costume similar to that of the contemporary post-boys.

Plate 9

Left: France, 1722. Captain of the *Cent-Suisses* (Hundred-Swiss) of the Royal Household under Louis XV (Marquis de Courtenvaux).

Engraving by Cochin, after A. Danchet, *Le Sacre de Louis XV dans l'Église de Reims*, Paris, 1722.

The guard known as the *Cent Suisses du Roy*, raised in 1497, accompanied and waited upon the King at all ceremonies at Versailles and Paris, and even acted as his escort in war. The gala dress, standardised from the 16th century, became blue, red and silver under Louis XIV and remained, apart from a few details, until 1830.

For ordinary duty, a blue uniform with red facings and silver lace replaced the archaic ceremonial dress with its slashes and ample breeches. The motto inscribed on its Colours was, "EA EST FIDUCIA GENTIS", which recalls the noble and famous device "Honour and Fidelity" borne by Swiss soldiers in foreign services.

These troops and their costume were imitated by the courts of Brandenburg, Saxony, Lorraine and other principalities.

Right: Electorate of Brandenburg, 1700. Ensign, from an engraving by Peter Schenk (1645–1715) published in a series of uniforms of the Guards of the Elector at Amsterdam.

This is the only hitherto unpublished print from that album, from which Kling and Knötel have reproduced most of the Guard uniforms.

In the Foot Guards, dressed in dark blue, the officers wore the gold-laced red coat after 1702, and it is even possible that this was worn as early as 1700.

Plate 10

Hessen-Darmstadt, c. 1786. Grenadiers. Anonymous drawing (Druène Collection, Paris).

The group depicted by the artist may belong to the Leib-Grenadier-Guard Regiment of the Landgrave Louis IX (1768–1790). The style of the uniform, copied from the Prussian model, still retains various features of the Seven Years War period.

Plate 11

United States of America, c. 1776.

Militiaman. Engraving by M. Will, Augsburg, c. 1778.

The soldier shown here, drawn from life for the first time by a contemporary, wears the light-coloured and fringed canvas clothing of a rifleman. The carbine is replaced by a bayonet-musket. The head-dress takes the form of a bishop's mitre, with a point front and back, as portrayed on an accompanying print, showing a side-view of the same figure. The mitre carries an indistinct inscription and a plume.

Plate 12

France, c. 1740. Dragoon on Forage Patrol. Engraving from "Mes Rêveries", by Maurice de Saxe. The Hague, 1756.

To find enough food for the cavalry horses was one of the major preoccupations of an army in the field, especially in the 18th century.

The close proximity of the enemy, with the ever-present danger of a surprise attack, made it necessary for the foragers to carry arms at all times.

The soldier shown here, probably a light dragoon dressed according to the ideas of Marshal de Saxe, simply wears a waistcoat, undress cap and breeches with stockings.

He is armed with a carbine, and a sickle hangs from his forage-bag. The horse-furniture and the sheepskin are in keeping with the innovations dear to Marshal de Saxe.

Plate 13

France, 1779. Alsace Infantry Regiment (German). Dillon Infantry Regiment (Irish), Royal-Allemand Cavalry, Bercheny Hussars. (From *État Général des Uniformes de toutes les Troupes de France par M.P.F. d'Isnard*, Strasbourg, 1779).

M.P.F. d'Isnard (1727–1807), a former cavalry officer at Strasbourg, was an engraver and first publisher of the Strasbourg "paper soldiers" between 1770 and 1790, an industry which flourished especially during the First Empire.

The particular copy of the publication used here appears to have been hand-coloured by the author, judging from certain details, such as the small plumes on the hats or the fringed epaulettes, which differ from the copies in the Bibliothèque Nationale in Paris and the library of Basle University.

The line troops depicted are foreign units in French service, recognisable particularly from the colour of their coat, e.g. "dark sky-blue" for the Germans and red for the Swiss and Irish. The "Royal Allemand Cavalry" was of German origin.

The foreign regiments disappeared with the Revolution. Some of them emigrated, such as the "Royal Allemand", which finally took service in Austria.

Bercheny's, a Hussar Regiment, the oldest of the French Hussar units, was dressed in sky-blue, and since it was raised in 1791 became the First Regiment of Hussars.

Plate 14

The water-colour painted by d'Isnard represents the full dress of the grenadier companies of the French and Swiss Guards, and (below) the *Gardes du Corps* and Gendarmes of the King's Household. These uniforms, profusely laced, were typical of the various guards units of the *Ancien Régime* disbanded at the Revolution.

Plate 15

France, 1796. Volunteer of the Army of the Rhine. Drawn from life by Benjamin Zix, 1796 (Print Room, Strasbourg).

The artist, Benjamin Zix (1772–1811), born at Strasbourg, left first-hand eye-witness records of the campaigns of 1793 to 1809 which are of great documentary value. The striking figure of a volunteer from the time of the Revolutionary Wars, returning in rags, but with bulging purse and haversack, is rendered here with the precision and perception of a great artist.

Plate 16

Left: Saxony, 1803. Hussar. Saxon Regiment of Hussars. Drawn from life and engraved by C. F. Holtzmann. Dresden, 1803.

Charles Frederick Holtzmann (1740–1811) was well-known in Dresden as an engraver and art teacher.

This Hussar regiment, raised in 1791, took part in the 1806 Campaign (Saalfeld) in the uniform shown here. In 1810 it received a sky-blue jacket with white braiding and a shako, and in 1822 was converted to a cavalry regiment.

Right: Austria, 1793. Officer of the Styrian Free Corps. This fine coloured engraving by Chrétien de Mechel (1737–1817), the well-known Basle engraver and publisher, is drawn from life.

Despite the oriental style of the uniform, it represents quite clearly an officer of Wurmser's Austrian Free Corps. The gold sword-knot proclaims the rank of officer. Raised in 1793, in Slavonia, near the Turkish frontier, this unit took part in the fighting in Alsace and was finally disbanded in 1801.

The uniform should have consisted of dark blue clothing with red piping, and red cloaks, but the disregard for dress regulations is clearly shown by this border-trooper's attire, in which only the cockade, the traditional oak-sprig and the sword knot indicate his Austrian nationality.

Plate 17

Officers of various European countries, *c.* 1802. Coloured engravings from an album by Fr. L. von Köller, Kiel, 1802.

Left: (1) The officer of Prussian Fusiliers of the Westphalian Brigade is still wearing the hat and coat which were regulation in 1797, and doubtless still worn later when off duty. The lining should be of green serge, which was changed to red in 1799. The facings were of crimson velvet for the officers. In 1797 the officers' dress sword was replaced by a light curved sabre.

(2) The French line infantry officer is distinguished by his curiously striped trousers.

(3) The Danish officer belongs to the Norwegian Guard Regiment and wears the red coat which has remained traditional in Denmark since 1700.

(4) The Hanoverian officer, wearing the scarlet coat familiar in Great Britain from the 17th century, belongs to the 4th Infantry Regiment.

Right: (1) Danish Lieutenant-General in a red coat with gold epaulettes and embroidery.

(2) The officer of Prussian Cuirassier Regiment No. 5 sports the white gala coat which was worn only on certain special occasions.

(3) The Portuguese infantry officer probably belongs to the 1st (Olivenca) Regiment. The crimson sash is still worn today by officers in full dress.

(4) The officer of the Netherlands Regiment of Walloon Dragoons is in a blue coat, introduced in 1752, and wears the orange "duty" sash.

Plate 33. Bombardment of Würzburg, 1813, by Austrian and Bavarian troops.

Plate 35, page 101. Baden, 1824. Officer of the *Garde du Corps.*

Plate 36, page 103. Left: Prussia, *c.* 1830. N.C.O. of the 2nd Foot Guard Regiment in full dress.

Right: Prussia, *c.* 1830. Pioneers of the Corps of Guard Engineers in service dress.

Russia, 1837. Non-commissioned officer of the 1st Landwehr Regiment is admired by the Civil Guard.

Saxony, c. 1820. Miners of Freiberg, blacksmith.

Plate 34. Saxony, c. 1820. Miners of Freiberg, musician in festival dress.

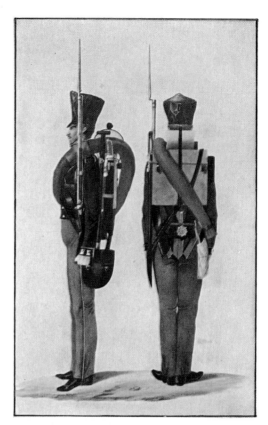

Plate 37. Bavaria, *c.* 1835. Prince Charles of Bavaria, Colonel
in chief of the 1st Cuirassier Regiment.

Plate 38. Great Britain, *c.* 1850. Officer of the 11th Hussar
Regiment in full dress.

Spain, c. 1845. Trumpeter and Lancer of the 1st Calatrava Lancer Regiment.

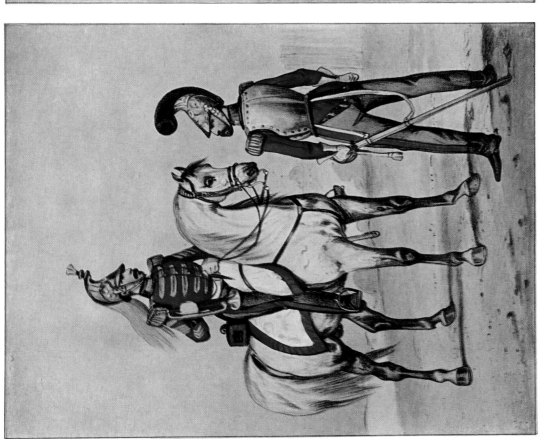

Plate 39. Spain, c. 1845. Trumpeter and Cuirassier of the 1st King's Cuirassier Regiment.

Plate 40. Prussia, 1845. Officer and Jaegers of the Guard.

Prussia, 1845. Infantry, Chasseurs and "Schützen". From left to right: 1. Private, 2. "Musketier", 3. "Schütze", 4. Chasseur of the Guard, 5. "Musketier", 6. Chasseur, 7. Grenadier, 8. N.C.O. of Fusiliers.

Plate 41. Prussia, *c.* 1830. Uhlans of the Guard (Landwehr).

Baden, 1834. Dragoons.

Plate 42. Prussia, *c.* 1833. N.C.O. of the Neuchâtel Rifle Battalion.

Plate 43. France, 1859. Parisian Firemen in action.

Plate 44, page 119. France, *c.* 1854. March Past of the Grenadiers Guard.

Plate 18

Great Britain, *c.* 1803. Naval Artillery. Coloured engraving by Mettenleitner, from the work by J. B. Seele, Volz, etc., on the armies of Europe. Augsburg, 1802–1809, Book V.

The artist has represented from left to right: three gunners, an officer laying a gun, a subaltern with a port-fire and two sailors. Great Britain was the first country to introduce a naval uniform for the ships' companies of men-o'-war, viz. blue with white facings. Epaulettes appeared from the middle of the 18th century, yet no regulations covered the style or colour of the ratings' dress. The sailors were distinguished from the gun crews by their short blue jackets.

Plate 19

France, *c.* 1805. Horse Artillery. Coloured engraving by Joh. Volz (same source as Plate 18).

Here are the main types of this branch, with a *Chef d'Escadron* in the centre. On the right, a gunner wearing a shako, and between the two an artillery driver in blue-grey and a bicorn. In the foreground a trumpeter in red breeches partly masks a gunner in a frock coat standing behind him. All are still wearing queues, a style of hair-dressing that was officially abolished in 1807 for the line regiments, although the Imperial Guard retained it until they were disbanded in 1815.

Plate 20

France, 1805. French Dragoon. Coloured engraving by J. B. Seele, Stuttgart, 1805. Jean Baptiste Seele (1774–1816) was Court painter and director of the Gallery of the Princes of Fürstenberg at Donaueschingen. He also worked at Stuttgart. A talented artist, engraver and lithographer, he is known more particularly for his plates of uniforms, military scenes and battle pictures.

This Dragoon, depicted during the war in Germany, and whose regiment cannot be identified, is shown in marching order. He wears the coatee and the red fringed epaulettes denoting the *élite* company of the regiment.

Plate 21

Austria, 1805. Hussar Regiment of Hessen-Homburg No. 4. Engraving, with unfinished colouring, by Adam von Bartsch, after Wilhelm von Kobell.

Wilhelm von Kobell (1776–1855) achieved fame as a painter at Mannheim, Düsseldorf, Vienna, Paris and Munich. He is distinguished especially for his many pictures of uniforms and battle scenes between 1800 and 1815.

Adam von Bartsch (1757–1821) worked as an engraver in Vienna and also acquired fame as a publisher.

The uniform shown here is that of the Austrian Hussar Regiment Hessen-Homburg No. 4, worn from 1767 with few changes until the first third of the 19th century.

The green colour of the pelisse shows up as yellow on the print, in the detachment on the march in the background. The saddle-cloths were red and identical for all Hussar regiments. The Imperial cypher F II (Francis II) was altered, after the fall of the Holy Roman Empire in 1806, to F I.

A sutleress is shown in the background in her picturesque national costume.

Plate 22

Austria, *c.* 1805. Infantry and Artillery. Water-colour (and cavalry counterpart) by W. v. Kobell (Charlottenburg Castle, Berlin).

For Wilhelm v. Kobell, see illustration above.

Apart from the infantry which occupies the central section of the picture, the group comprises a party of gunners on the left, with artillery and transport officers.

A general—recognisable by his red breeches and the green plume on his hat—is accompanied by a group of infantry officers wearing the crested helmet introduced in 1798. This disappeared in 1808, to be replaced by the shako already shown on two of the officers here. On the right are some grenadiers wearing the bearskin cap and belonging to German and Hungarian regiments. The Hungarians wear the characteristic sky-blue trousers.

Plate 23

Austria, *c.* 1805. *Chevaulégers*, Regiment Hessen-Homburg No. 2. Coloured engraving by J. B. Seele entitled "The Chance Meeting".

Some regiments of Austrian dragoons had been converted to *chevaulégers*, wearing a uniform in the same style as previously, except for the colour, which was changed from white to green.

This regiment was raised in 1758 under the name of Löwenstein-Wertheim Dragoons. It fought in the Tyrol in 1805, in Italy in 1809 and distinguished itself in the retreat to Carinthia.

When it was converted to light dragoons the regiment wore a white uniform with dark green facings from 1802 to 1805, but reverted at its own request to the green uniform worn prior to 1802.

Plate 24

Above: Prussia. Left: Officer and other rank of the King's Regiment No. 18, *c.* 1800. Engraving by G. L. Ramm, from an album of uniforms. Berlin, 1800. Officials of the Water and Forestry Department (*centre*) and the Post Office, 1787 (*right*). Taken from C. Horvath's album of Prussian civil service uniforms, Potsdam, 1787.

The revival of the classical tricorn in the Prussian infantry, which replaced the bicorn in 1798, restored the general appearance of the Prussian soldier to that of the later years of Frederick the Great. The distinctive lacing remained unaltered and was omitted only in field service dress. The remains of this regiment, either dismissed or disbanded at the capitulation of Prenzlau, rejoined the Regiment of Foot Guards in 1806.

The uniforms of civil servants bore a very close resemblance to the dress of the officers in the 18th-century army, except that the distinctive attributes of a Prussian officer (silver thread sash and sword-knot) were substituted, in the case of civil servants, for epaulettes in the French style by Frederick William II. The green coats of the Foresters and the blue of the Post Office officials were made regulation and compulsory as early as the 18th century.

Below: Prussia, 1806. Carabinier of Leibhussar Regiment von Rudorff No. 2 (*left*) and Grenadier non-commissioned officer of Grenadier Battalion von Reinbaben, Larisch Infantry Regiment No. 26 (*right*).

Engravings by W. Henschel from the Prussian Army album published by Schiavonetti, Berlin, 1806. Wilhelm Henschel (1781–1865) and his brother Moritz worked in Berlin as engravers and artists. They were the authors of the well-known collection of uniforms of the French Imperial Guard at Berlin, drawn from life in 1807.

The drawings shown here were prepared shortly before the destruction of the old Prussian Army and show the smart though impractical uniform of that body. Admittedly, improvements were in hand, but only a few units were to benefit before the outbreak of war.

The Carabinier, armed with the rifled carbine of the cavalry regiments, is already wearing the new 1805 shako, then gradually replacing the mirliton still in use. The white plume with black centre denotes a carabinier. This celebrated old von Zieten Hussar regiment was disbanded after the Capitulation of Ratkau in 1806.

The Grenadier non-commissioned officer of Larisch Regiment No. 26 carries a spontoon, and wears a cane, gloves and a black-topped plume. The cuffs and the band on his head-dress are edged with gold lace. The scarlet lapels are buttoned and turned back at the top. Grey canvas trousers covered the breeches and gaiters in field service dress.

Plate 25

Prussia, 1806: Officer of the *Garde du Corps* Regiment. Coloured engraving from the album by W. Henschel, Berlin, 1806.

Raised in 1740, this cavalry unit was the most aristocratic of the whole Prussian Army under the monarchy. The officer shown here is wearing full dress. The basic colour of the coat—at first pale yellow—finally became white towards the end of the 18th century, in common with all the other cuirassier regiments except the Second,

which retained the yellow colouring until 1809. The cuirasses were discarded in 1709. The bicorn and its plume, just before the war of 1806, had reached such exaggerated proportions as to cause real discomfort to the wearer, since the leather chinstrap was not introduced until the beginning of the campaign. The active service sword of the regiment carried a silver-plated hilt until 1798.

Plate 26

French Troops at Lübeck, 1806. Coloured engraving by Chr. Gottfried Geissler (1770–1844), well known for his engravings of battle scenes at Leipzig between 1806 and 1813.

This little-known print represents an episode in the taking of Lübeck on 6th November, 1806. The French troops entering the town are engaged in street fighting.

In the foreground a quarrel appears to have arisen concerning the safety of a baby held by a French Hussar of the 6th Regiment (?), a *Chasseur à Cheval* (back view) and an officer of the Polish Legion (?) on his fallen horse. In the background, an officer of Blücher's Prussian Hussar Regiment No. 8 is struck by a bullet, while on the right a light infantryman of the 96th French Infantry of the Line runs forward. He wears the greatcoat and a bicorn, which was replaced in the following year by the stiff shako.

Plate 27

Left: Spain, 1807. Sutleress and musician of the Catalonian Infantry Regiment.

The Romana Division, sent from Spain to form part of the Grand Army, created a favourable impression during its stay in Hamburg, not only because of its attractive national uniforms but also because of its bearing and discipline.

Accompanied by a very large baggage train—and even by wives and children—the soldiers preserved their uniforms by wearing civilian clothing in camp and on the march.

The sutleress and musician above wear their national costume, including fan and umbrella.

Right: Trooper of the Algarve Regiment with his wife. Wearing his drill clothing and pointed undress cap, the man rides side-saddle and carries in front of him his sky-blue uniform with white cuffs. His companion is in full national costume and wears the top hat no doubt belonging to her husband.

Centre: France, *c.* 1810. Drummer of Customs Units.

In order to enforce the continental blockade, Hamburg received a number of military customs units within its walls. The drummer shown here, obviously caricatured, wears an enormous bicorn with a colossal blue–red–white plume. This was the correct order for the French national colours in those days, which were standardised in 1812 as blue–white–red.

This drawing is by Christoph Suhr; see notes to Plate 29.

Plate 28

Left: France, 1812/13. New Guard of the 1st Cuirassier Regiment at Hamburg. These are shown in dismounted order, armed with a bayonet-carbine, and without cuirasses. Behind the trumpeter is a warrant officer with drawn sword and white pouch. The last man wears gaiters instead of boots.

Right: France, 1812/13. Officers and Eagle-bearer of the 93rd Regiment of Infantry of the Line.

The two grenadier officers are still wearing the bear-skin cap, with different plates, which had been officially abolished. The officer in the bicorn has a sabre (broken in action?), while the others wear swords.

The Eagle-bearer holds the staff surmounted by the regulation eagle and bearing a purple ribbon. The symbolic nature of the flag was not represented by the silk but by the metal eagle at the head of the staff. On active service, or on the march, the silk was often entrusted to the care of the Commanding Officer, as were the regimental funds. Drawings by Christoph Suhr; see notes to Plate 29.

Plate 29

Above: France, 1813.

"Seamen on the Alster" at Hamburg. The dearth of occupation troops and the failure of the French Navy at sea prompted the employment of sea-going personnel on land. A captain in a coatee heads a detachment from an *élite* unit wearing oilskin hats with an anchor badge. A red waistcoat seems to be worn under the navy-blue jacket; and a young drummer marches at the head of the group.

Below: *Élite* troops of a *Chasseurs à Cheval* regiment of the same period, led by an officer. The indistinct colouring of the facings may be either orange or salmon pink (*aurore*), and therefore makes it impossible to identify the unit accurately. The red plumes on the bearskin caps, and the red-fringed epaulettes, are typical of *élite* units. Pioneers, carrying lances, are on the right wing; they are also recognised by the crossed-axes insignia on the right arm. The officer is recognisable, among other distinctions, by his grey overalls.

Drawings by Christoph Suhr.

Christoph Suhr, art master (1771–1842) and his brother Cornelius (1781–1857) worked at Hamburg and were known as black-and-white artists, painters and lithographers. The elder spent much time, with the help of his younger brother, compiling a record of the many occupation troops passing through Hamburg between 1806 and 1815. These drawings, made on the spot, are of considerable documentary value, although it is not always possible to date them with accuracy. The collection, showing the troops stationed at Hamburg, and commonly known in France as the "Bourgeois de Hamburg" book, has provided these reproductions (Plates 27–30), which are taken from one of the very rare original copies still in existence.

Plate 30

Holland, *c.* 1810. 6th Infantry Regiment at Hamburg.

Suhr devotes two pages to various types of this unit.

From left to right: a grenadier pennant-bearer of the 2nd Battalion; a grenadier officer; two pioneers, and the Drum Major preceding fifers from the fusilier and grenadier companies.

This uniform, designed in 1806 at the time of the formation of the Kingdom of the Netherlands, was white for infantry regiments, with contrasting facing colours (light green for the 6th).

The plumes are in the old Dutch colours instead of red, and the bearskin caps are fitted with scaled chin-straps tied up behind the cap, while the hair is plaited and forms a queue. The blue clothing of the pioneers appears to have been drawn from existing stores pending the issue of replacements. The Drum Major's dress is generously laced, and he wears, in addition to his plumed bicorn, the same "swallows' nests" as the musicians. Drawing by Christoph Suhr; see notes to Plate 29.

Plates 31 and 32

Kingdom of Westphalia, 1810.

Plate 31: Lieutenant-Colonel of the *Garde du Corps*, full dress (mounted).

Plate 32: Captain-General of the Guard in levée dress (*left*) and *Chasseur-Carabinier* (*right*), all from the album by Alexander Sauerweid, 1810.

Alexander Sauerweid (1782–1844), black-and-white artist and engraver, first at Dresden, then, from 1811, at St. Petersburg. Celebrated for his military prints and accurate attention to detail.

The *Garde du Corps*, raised in 1810 for special service with King Jerome, was a single company entrusted with palace duties at Kassel, and provided the Royal escort. The other ranks consisted in the main of former Polish Lancers who had accompanied Jerome to his new capital. They never saw active service.

The Captains-General of the Guard took turns in duty-in-waiting with the King and the Guard, the officer on duty assuming the functions of Commanding Officer of the Guard.

The corps of *Chasseurs-Carabiniers*, formed originally from foresters, consisted of four companies responsible, in peace-time, for work in the Royal forests. In time of war they served as light infantry, and were the only unit to be armed with rifled carbines.

The uniform, like the entire organisation of the Westphalian Army, was based upon the French model. The luxurious uniforms of the Guard and Court were based on the King's personal tastes, while all the infantry was dressed in white, in uniforms and head-dresses of French design.

Plate 33

Bombardment of Würzburg, 1813.
Coloured engraving by Adam von Bartsch, after Wilhelm von Kobell.

Austrian and Bavarian troops advance towards the besieged city. A regiment of Austrian dragoons, with the regulation black-and-yellow crests removed from their helmets, appears on the left, escorting an Austrian baggage wagon whose drivers wear the characteristic blue-grey uniform.

Advancing in the centre are two grenadiers, the one on the left from a "German" regiment with white breeches and greatcoat; the other a Hungarian with tight blue trousers. A Bavarian *Chevauléger* of the 4th or 5th Regiment trots between two Austrian dragoons, while a Bavarian infantryman walks on the right. In the background, Bavarian–Austrian staff officers direct operations.

Plate 34

Saxony, *c.* 1820. Freiberg Miners.
Coloured plate from the album of miners' costumes of the Kingdom of Saxony. Freiberg, *c.* 1820.

The full dress worn by the miners in most of the mining provinces of Germany displays a particular affinity with military uniforms.

The miner shown here wears working clothes, while the musician is in festive dress.

This costume—which was subject to regulation in some districts after the middle of the 18th century—was completed by the curious peakless shako and its plume. The knees were protected by aprons or leather knee-pieces. When marching, or in procession, the miners carried axes with slender handles.

This costume is still worn today in the mining districts of Germany, Austria and Alsace.

Plate 35

Baden, 1824. Officer of the *Garde du Corps*. Lithograph by J. Voellinger from the album of uniforms of the Grand Duchy of Baden, Karlsruhe, 1824.

This regiment, raised as a palace guard in the 18th century, received a Prussian-type uniform in 1819 and was incorporated in 1833 in the Regiment of Dragoons of the Guard. It then assumed the dress of that unit.

Plate 36

Left: Prussia, *c.* 1830. Non-commissioned officer of the 2nd Foot Guard Regiment in full dress. Coloured lithograph by Jügel after a drawing by Friedrich Lieder.

The 2nd Foot Guard Regiment was raised in 1813 from an ordinary training battalion formed in 1811, which then assumed the uniform of that unit, viz., a Guards uniform, but with gold buttons and lace. The cuffs were first worn closed and were red, like the shoulder-straps. The cuff-slash was blue. It was not until 1834 that the regiment was granted open cuffs with loops.

Right: Prussia, *c.* 1830. Pioneers of the Corps of Guard Engineers in service dress. Coloured lithograph by Jügel after Lieder.

The engineering branch of the Prussian Army, only created in 1810, shows its artillery connection by its black collar and cuffs. The Corps of Guard Engineers consisted, until 1816, of the Brandenburg Pioneers and the 5th Company of Field Pioneers.

The shoulder-straps, originally black, became red for the Guard in 1816, and in 1830 for all engineer units. The broad saw-bladed swords were carried on the pack with the remainder of the engineering tools.

In 1830 a section of optical telegraphists was attached to the Guard Engineers, but was discontinued in 1833.

From 1823 the corps supplied a small unit of boatmen for the Royal craft on the Potsdam canals. This was incorporated in the new Royal Navy in 1849.

Below: Prussia, 1837. Non-commissioned officers of the 1st Landwehr Regiment of the Guard. Coloured lithograph by Mittag, after L. Elsholtz, 1837. Citizens typically dressed as part-time soldiers admire a non-commissioned officer of the Guard Landwehr in service dress.

The shako is covered by its protective oilskin and the greatcoat is worn bandolier-fashion in the typical Prussian manner.

Plate 37

Bavaria, *c.* 1835. Prince Charles of Bavaria, Colonel of the 1st Cuirassier Regiment at Munich. Coloured lithograph by S. Krauss, Munich.

This regiment was raised in 1815 under the command of Prince Charles, and in 1825 amalgamated with the former *Gardes du Corps* and the 2nd Cuirassiers, also raised in 1815.

The new regiment, renamed the First, assumed white metal buttons, but the large early-model crested helmet was replaced by a lighter head-dress. The white breeches disappeared between 1829 and 1832 to be replaced by blue overalls with red piping, which was altered to a red band in 1834. The saddle-cloth was blue after 1830. Finally, the 1st and 2nd Regiments were distinguished only by the buttons: white metal for the 1st and brass for the 2nd. In 1879 both were converted to heavy cavalry without cuirasses.

The 1st Regiment is shown here in full dress, headed by the Commanding Officer, ready to march past, while the band, mounted on greys, is commanded by the Trumpet-Major wearing the silver stripes of a non-commissioned officer and mounted on a bay.

Plate 38

Great Britain, c. 1850. Officer of the 11th (Prince Albert's Own) Hussars in full dress. Coloured lithograph by R. Ackermann, London, 1840–58.

This field officer is shown in a dark blue jacket and pelisse, trimmed with gold lace, and the well-known "cherry-red" overalls. In 1840, after providing the escort for Prince Albert (The Prince Consort) when he landed at Dover, they were honoured with their present title. They took part in the famous Charge of the Light Brigade at Balaclava during the Crimean War in 1854. The traditional "cherry-red" overalls are still worn today on special occasions.

Plate 39

Spain, c. 1845. Left: Trumpeter and Cuirassier of the 1st King's Cuirassier Regiment.

Right: Trumpeter and Lancer, 1st Calatrava Lancer Regiment.

After the album by D. J. Villagas; lithographs by V. Adam. Madrid, 1846. Victor Adam (1801–1866) worked in Paris as a painter of battle scenes and lithographer.

These Spanish cavalry uniforms of the mid-19th century show the marked French influence of the period.

Plate 40

Above: Prussia, 1845. Jaegers of the Guard.

Below: Prussia, 1845. Infantry and Jaegers. Anonymous coloured lithographs. With the introduction of the tunic and *pickelhaube* in October, 1842, the Prussian infantry assumed that characteristic appearance which was to remain until 1914, and was imitated by other countries.

The officer and the Jaegers of the Guard wear the spiked helmet, which was replaced only in 1854 by the double-peaked shako. The rolled greatcoat carried bandolier-fashion is typical of the Prussian Army. In winter black trousers with red piping replaced the white trousers worn in summer.

The lower plate represents the following units (from left to right):

1. Private of the Reserve Regiment of Landwehr-Guards.
2. 'Musketier' of the 20th Landwehr-Regiment.
3. Skirmisher of the 4th Detachment of Skirmishers.
4. Rifleman of the Battalion of Jaegers of the Guard.

5. 'Musketier' of the 2nd (The King's) Infantry Regiment.
6. Rifleman of the 3rd Detachment of Jaegers.
7. Grenadier of the 1st Regiment of Foot Guards.
8. Battalion company non-commissioned officer of Emperor Alexander's Regiment of Grenadiers.

Both plates show the typical uniform worn by Prussian Infantry up to 1848/49. The tunic varied little after that, but the helmet was shortened, first in 1857, and finally assumed the well-known shape of the pre-1914 era.

Plate 41

Above: Prussia, c. 1830. Regiment of Uhlans of the Guard (Landwehr).

Pencil drawing by von Elsholtz.

This picture shows, from left to right, a non-commissioned officer in duty dress; a field officer wearing a bicorn and another in full dress; an Uhlan in duty dress and an Uhlan and trumpeter in field-service dress.

This unit, raised in 1819, was divided into two regiments which, in 1826, became designated as the 1st and 2nd Regiments of Uhlans of the Guard (Landwehr).

The uniform was identical for both units, except that the buttons and lace were white for the first and yellow for the second. At first, the collars and cuffs varied according to squadrons, i.e., 1st white, 2nd red, 3rd yellow, 4th sky-blue, and crimson for headquarters. They were altered to red for both regiments in 1851.

Below: Dragoons of the Grand Duchy of Baden, 1834. Engraving by R. Kuntz. The three dragoon regiments in existence after 1815 received a new uniform in 1834: sky-blue with brass buttons, sky-blue overalls with white stripes and leather grips, white collar, cuffs and piping. Regimental distinctions were worn on the shoulder-straps in the form of a crown for the Grand Duke's Regiment and numerals 1 and 2 for the two others. The saddle-cloths were sky-blue with white ornaments.

This print shows rankers in various orders of dress, a trumpeter in a striped uniform, three officers (*centre*) and a Dragoon in field-service dress.

Plate 42

Prussia, c. 1833. Non-commissioned officer of the Neuchâtel Rifle Battalion (*Garde-Schützen*). Lithograph by Sebbers.

Raised in June, 1814, at Neuchâtel (Switzerland) from the remains of the Neuchâtel Battalion in French service, this unit was brought up to establishment by recruits from the Principality and from Valengin: The battalion, stationed at Berlin, was noted for its special origins and traditions.

The uniform was the same as for the Silesian Battalion, except that the epaulettes were bright red and the black collar was trimmed with yellow lace. In 1816, as a special distinction, the battalion was given cuff-slashes in the French style, instead of the straight slashes worn by the Prussian infantry.

Plate 43

France, 1859. Paris Firemen in action.

Sergeant and officer. Lithograph from "Uniformes de l'Armée Française en 1861 . . ." by Armand Dumaresq, Paris, 1861.

Edouard Armand Dumaresq (1826–95) of Paris, was much admired for his military drawings and battle pictures. Employed as an artist by the War Ministry, he left an important collection of drawings of contemporary uniforms.

Created in 1811, the military Regiment of Sapper-Firemen of Paris was formed by the Fire Guards of the City at a strength of one battalion, which became a regiment in 1865.

For all reviews, and in full dress, this unit wore military uniform and equipment, but for fire duty the dress was adapted to circumstances.

The traditional uniform was dark blue with red facings, blue-grey trousers with red piping and a helmet bearing a red plume when full dress was ordered.

The regiment acquired a fine reputation for discipline and devotion to duty on countless occasions involving fire-fighting and rescue work.

Plate 44

France, c. 1854. March Past of the Grenadiers of the Imperial Guard. Woodcut from the *Illustrated London News*, 1854 (Druène Collection, Paris). The slow march, in three ranks, is depicted splendidly in this picture by an unknown artist, emphasising the striking and colourful effect of a body of soldiers moving in unison.

For notes on this uniform, see Plate 50 (*right*).

Plate 45

France, 1848. Trooper of the Republican Guard of Paris.

Coloured lithograph by Victor Adam.

Victor Adam (1801–66), born and died in Paris, is known for his many lithographs and military paintings.

The Municipal Guard of Paris was dismissed in 1848, after the political upheavals of the times, and replaced by a corps of volunteers, 600 strong, under the name of *Garde Républicaine de l'Hotel de Ville* (Town Hall Republican Guard). This, in turn was disbanded on 27th May, 1848, to be replaced by the Parisian Republican Guard.

The uniform shown here was worn after the first raising of volunteers, and includes the blue smock with red scarf and belt, which was replaced soon afterwards by a dress of more marked military design.

Plate 46

Austria, 1848.
Above: Captain of *Seressaners*, Uhlans and Borderers.
Below: Border troops.
Coloured lithographs by Girolamo Franceschini and Höfelich, Vienna, 1848.

G. Franceschini (1820–59), whose family originated in Trieste, was a black-and-white artist and lithographer. He became Director of Costume to the two Court Theatres of Vienna and is known particularly for his prints of Austrian and Hungarian uniforms.

The first print represents Albert Jelachich von Buzim, a captain in the Corps of *Seressaners* in 1848. He is wearing the typical national costume of the "Red-Cloaks" and should not be mistaken for the *Banus* of Croatia, Joseph Jellacic von Buzim.

Every border regiment of infantry was accompanied by a corps of *Seressaners*. These were irregular troops, employed on police duties in peace-time, but serving as staff guides during the campaigns of 1848/49.

Behind the captain stands an Uhlan of the Galician Regiment Count Civalart No. 1. This regiment fought at Prague and Vienna in 1848, and against Hungary in the following year.

On the left, a *Seressaner* and an infantryman of Border Regiment No. 4 or 6, wearing on the cuffs the "bear's-paw" type of loop and the tight breeches peculiar to the Hungarian units:

Below: Austria, 1848.
The Border troops on this plate show a typical example of the disregard for regulation dress caused by the exigencies of active service.

From left to right:

1. Border Infantry Regiment No. 1 (Liccaner).
2. *Banderial* Hussar.
3. Infantryman of Warasdin St. George Border Regiment No. 6, 4th Battalion.
4. Border Gunner of the 4th Battalion.
5. and 6. Two "Red-Cloaks" (seated and standing).
7. 2nd Battalion, Gradisca Border Infantry Regiment No. 8.

Apart from the infantryman on the right, in regulation dress, a patent lack of orderliness appears in the other types represented here. These units were rapidly embodied, as and when events required.

The Hussars were raised in July, 1848, in Croatia, taking part in the fighting in Vienna in 1848 and in Hungary in 1849 against the insurgents. In 1851 this unit became Count Wallmoden-Gimborn's Uhlan Regiment No. 5.

Plate 47

Russia, c. 1850. Division of Cuirassiers of the Guard.
Contemporary coloured lithograph after A. Ladurner (Historical Museum, Rastatt).

From left to right:

1. Gendarme of the Guard in full dress.
2. Mounted Guard in *soubreveste* (dress cuirass).
3. The Empress's Chevalier-Guards. Non-commissioned officers in full dress.
4. The Empress's Chevalier-Guard in *soubreveste*.
5. The hereditary Grand-Duke's Cuirassier Regiment in full dress.
6. The Empress's Chevalier-Guards. Service dress with lance (front rank).
7. Mounted Guard in full dress.
8. Cuirassier of the Emperor's Regiment. Service dress with lance.
9. Horse Artillery.

With the introduction of the Prussian-type helmet in 1846, the Russian cuirassiers assumed an almost Prussian appearance, an influence, incidentally, which persisted in the full dress of the Cavalry of the Guard, until 1914.

When all the cavalry was converted to Dragoons in 1882, the Cavalry of the Guard retained its old prerogatives.

Plate 48

Above: Kingdom of Sardinia, 1854. General commanding the Expeditionary Force in the Crimea.

Coloured lithograph by V. Grassier-Valetti, showing the Piedmontese in the Crimea, Turin, 1855.

General Alphonso La Marmora followed by his staff. On the right, an officer of the Nizza Cavalry Regiment in a crested helmet. The white cross of the House of Savoy is worn here as a national badge on head-dresses and equipment. The uniforms are based upon the French pattern, clearly perceptible in the infantry wearing shako and greatcoat.

Below: Russia, *c.* 1850. Horse Grenadiers of the Guard.

Coloured lithograph taken from the "Album Militaire Russe" by A. Charlemagne, Moscow and St. Petersburg, undated (Historical Museum, Rastatt).

The characteristic colour is still dark green. The grenadiers are wearing the fringed epaulettes of *élite* troops and the curious fur-crested helmet already in use under the Empress Catherine II in 1786. The mounted drummer, recalling as such the former dragoon status of the Regiment, is distinguished by the red crest on his helmet and the profuse lacing of his uniform.

Plate 49

Austria, 1854. Marine Infantry. Coloured lithograph from the book by Pettenkofer and Strassgechwandtner on the Austrian Army, Vienna, 1854.

From left to right, the group represents rank and file in full dress, wearing the tunic introduced in 1851, with red facings and characteristic epaulettes of the Austro-Hungarian Army.

A captain, second-Lieutenant and surgeon in a bicorn make up the centre portion, while some gunners appear in the background. For a great many years this branch was recruited in the Italian provinces of the former Empire, and orders were given in Italian.

After having been disbanded in 1848 for insubordination, the Corps was fully reorganised in 1849 and merged into a single regiment in 1852. It was finally disbanded in 1871.

Plates 50 and 51

France, 1859. Plate 50: Corporal of Marines and ship's boy (*left*).—*Cantinière* and Drummer of a Regiment of Grenadiers of the Guard (*right*).

Plate 51: *Cantinière* and Lancer of the Regiment of Lancers of the Imperial Guard.

Coloured lithographs from H. Lalaisse, *Types Militaires du Troupier Français* and *L'Armée Française et ses Cantinières*. Paris, 1859. Hippolyte F. Lalaisse (1812–84) was born at Nancy and became a pupil of N. I. Charlet in Paris. As a painter and lithographer he is numbered among the best authorities on French uniforms between 1840 and 1870.

Plate 50 (*left*): The Marine Infantry was raised primarily for colonial service, and was distinguished from the infantry of the line by yellow-fringed epaulettes and blue trousers with a red band. The uniform shown here was introduced in 1845 and retained its special features when the Corps was converted to Colonial Infantry.

Plate 50 (*right*): Instituted in 1854, the Imperial Guard included three regiments of Foot Grenadiers, who first wore blue trousers, which were changed to red soon afterwards. The bearskin cap, bearing an eagle, and embellished with cords and a plume, was worn without any ornaments in field-service dress, which included the blue-grey greatcoat. This uniform was replaced in 1860 by a tunic with white loops.

The *cantinières*, or sutleresses, attached to the various regiments were distinguished, on full-dress occasions, by a costume specially designed in the colours of their unit. These women accompanied their regiments on active service and displayed exemplary courage.

Plate 51: The Regiment of Lancers of the Guard was raised in 1855 and dressed in a colourful uniform comprising a white *kurtka* with a blue *plastron*. The eight regiments of lancers of the line wore the same uniform but in blue, with various colours for the *plastron*, cuffs and turnbacks.

Plate 52

Above: Bavaria, 1854. Bavarian Royal Corps of Archers.

Coloured lithograph by L. Behringer, Munich, 1854.

The origin of this corps goes back to 1580, when it was a Carabinier Guard. It was subsequently constituted as the Archer Bodyguard in 1669. As Guards of the Elector of Bavaria, these troops took part in the Battle of Prague in 1620, which is commemorated in the point of their standard, showing the Virgin Mary and the Bavarian arms with the inscription "Augustae reliquiae victoriae Pragensis".

In the 18th century the Archers' functions became restricted to Court duties alone, charged with internal security service of the palace. They were disbanded in 1918.

The uniform retained the essential features of the 18th century, and the queue was not abolished until 1825. The type shown here, with helmet and tunic, dates only from 1852. The helmet was fitted with a plume for ordinary duty and a lion for gala occasions. The personal armament, a *couse*, goes back to the 16th century.

Below: Prussia, 1862. Cuirassier and Dragoon Officers. Chromo-lithograph by Anton von Werner and R. Meinhardt.

Anton von Werner (1843–1915) was well known in Berlin as an artist of historical subjects and contemporary illustrator.

From left to right:

1. Officer of Cuirassier Regiment No. 5 in levée dress.
2. Trooper of the *Gardes du Corps* Regiment in *soubreveste*.
3. Officer of the same regiment in ordinary Court dress.
4. Officer of the Cuirassiers of the Guard in levée dress.
5. Officer of Cuirassier Regiment No. 3 in evening dress.
6. Officer of Cuirassier Regiment No. 6 in interim dress.
7. Field officer of the 1st Regiment of Dragoons of the Guard in Court dress.
8. Officer of Dragoon Regiment No. 4 in levée dress.
9. Officer of Regiment No. 3 in interim dress.

The new regulations promulgated in 1842 specified a blue tunic for Dragoons and white for the Cuirassiers. They also governed the general appearance of these troops up to 1914, apart from a few minor details. The officers of the *Gardes du Corps* reverted to their 18th-century red uniform in 1842, but the Cuirassiers of the Guard did not follow suit until 1862.

1842 is also the date at which the gala *soubreveste* (or "drawing-room cuirass") was revived, having been discarded since the death of Frederick the Great. The sabretache did not reappear until 1883. The helmets of both regiments were fitted, after 1843, with a detachable silver eagle, which was not worn by the trumpeters until 1890.

On ballroom occasions at Court the dancers laid aside their pouches and sashes. This print shows in particular the changes ordered in 1862.

128

PICTURE ACKNOWLEDGEMENTS

Art Library of the former State Museums, Berlin:
Front and back end-papers;
Plates 1, 2, 3, 5, 6, 7, 9, 11, 13, 14, 16, 17, 19, 20, 21, 23, 24, 25, 26, 27, 28, 29, 30, 31, 32, 33, 34, 36, 37, 38, 40, 41 (top), 43, 45, 49, 50, 51

Historical Museum, Rastatt:
Plates 4, 39, 41 (bottom), 46, 47, 48

Municipal Museums, Strasbourg:
Plates 12, 15

Historical Museum, Basle (Photograph: Schwitter AG., Basle):
Plate 8

Administration of the former State Castles and Parks, Charlottenburg Palace, Berlin-Charlottenburg:
Plate 22

Former State Museums, Cabinet of copper-plate engravings, Berlin-Dahlem:
Plate 42

Rolf Keller, Stuttgart:
Plate 35

Hans-Joachim Ullrich, Berlin:
Plate 2 (bottom left)

Colonel Bernard Druène, Paris:
Plates 10, 44

The drawings in the text are by the author.

Plate 45. France, 1848. Trooper of the Parisian Republican Guard.

Plate 46, page 131. Above: Austria, 1848. From right to left: Captain of Seressans, Lancer, Border Infantry, Seressan Borderer.

Below: Austria, 1848. Border troops. From left to right: 1. Liccan Borderers, 2. *Banderial* Hussar, 3. Infantryman of Warasdin St. George Borderers, 4. Border Artillery, 5. Seressan Borderer (seated), 6. Seressan Borderer (standing), 7. Gradisca Border Infantry Regiment.

Plate 47, page 133. Russia, *c.* 1850. Division of Cuirassiers of the Guard.

Plate 48. Kingdom of Sardinia, 1854. General commanding the Expeditionary Force in the Crimea.

Russia, *c.* 1850. Horse Grenadiers of the Guard.

Plate 49, page 137. Austria, 1854. Marine Infantry; in the foreground a Captain (*left*), a Second-Lieutenant (*centre*) and a Surgeon (*right*).

Plate 51, page 141. France, 1859. *Cantinière* and Lancer of the Imperial Guard.

Plate 52, page 143. Above: Bavaria, 1854. Bavarian Royal Corps of Archers.

Below: Prussia, 1862. Cuirassier and Dragoon Officers.

France, 1859. *Cantinière* and drummer of the Grenadiers of the Guard.

Plate 50. France, 1859. Corporal of Marines and ship's boy.